GW00836120

The Symphony: From Mannheim to Mahler

CHRISTOPHER TARRANT AND NATALIE WILD

© 2022 by Christopher Tarrant and Natalie Wild

All rights administered worldwide by Faber Music Ltd

Bloomsbury House 74–77 Great Russell Street London WC1B 3DA

Music processed by Donald Thomson

Cover designed by Chloë Alexander

Text designed by Agnesi Text

Printed in England by Caligraving Ltd

All rights reserved

ISBN10: 0-571-54240-9

EAN13: 978-0-571-54240-6

Cover image:

The orchestra (Gustav Mahler conducting the Vienna Philharmonic Orchestra)

by Max Oppenheimer 1923

(Photo by Imagno/Getty Images)

Contents

To all music teachers and educators,
especially those who helped to shape our own musical development:
Sarah Brown, Peter Burbridge, J.P.E. Harper-Scott, Jane Higgins, Pearl Mace,
Nikki Rogers, Keith Smith and Graham Tear.

In memory of Alan Broadbent, whose generosity, charisma
and energetic passion inspired generations of musicians.

Foreword

The idea for this book came from a chance conversation between the two authors – one an academic, one a teacher – about the challenges facing music education. A review of teaching materials suggested that symphonic repertoire from the eighteenth and nineteenth centuries, which takes up substantial space in A-level syllabi, is largely taught chronologically, without a critical angle, and without teaching students to draw together contexts, materials, and ideas. The ethos of this project has been to build a connection between cutting-edge, academically rigorous ideas and practical, pedagogically informed communicative strategies. Inevitably, compromises have to be made in terms both of content and structure in order to create a one-volume introduction to such a broad subject. Our hope is that the chapters contained in this volume will not be read as the final word, but rather an opening-up and opening-out of a subject that readers will continue to pursue independently.

The structure of the book, while chronological in certain limited respects, approaches different topics related to symphonic composition in a way that reflects recent academic debates about instrumental music in the eighteenth and nineteenth centuries. In discussions of a topic that spans a century and a half, the trap is to lapse into purely chronological description, and a Whig view of history. The idea of constant progress is resisted in this book, along with the idea that the symphony was a stable category in the 150-year period under discussion. We have tried to give fair emphasis not just to the continuities and the sense of progression and development during this time, but also the discontinuities and ruptures that have characterised the genre, especially in the nineteenth century, while also shining a light on marginalised composers forgotten by history.

We have attempted to strike a balance between idealist and materialist approaches to this topic. A material study of the symphony includes all the obvious concrete objects that bring the genre to life: instruments, concert halls, printed music, published scores, and the like. We are also crucially and critically interested in musical materials – the 'stuff' of composition – which includes things like melodies, textures, cadences, and forms. These materials contrast with the much grander 'ideas' which have propagated, supported, fuelled, shaped and challenged the enterprise of symphonic composition; such ideas as nationalism, programmaticism, historicism, and the canon have all had an impact. The two approaches – one concerned with materials, which we focus on in Part II of the book, and the other focusing on contexts and ideas, which forms much of Parts I and III – are interdependent. One cannot succeed without the other.

This tension, which was articulated by Carl Dahlhaus in 1983, helps us to frame one of the central issues of so-called 'historical music' and its 'relevance' in the third decade of the twenty-first century.[1] Much of this music, particularly in the earlier stages of its development, would have been created and performed simply for the enjoyment of the wealthy and the powerful, and as a means for them to project their wealth and power. For much eighteenth-century orchestral music this is simply a truism, and one that has been used by some as a lever in an attempt to discredit the entire pursuit of performing, listening to, and studying this repertoire as elitist. The problem with this view is that this music is not simply an historical artefact. The strange thing about pieces of music is that they can be brought into life again and again. Pieces of music endure. They were created at a specific historical moment, but they have the unique ability to transcend epochs: they appear to us now, here in the present, and it is our responsibility to try to understand them and to bring all the knowledge that has accrued since the time of composition in order to broaden and deepen that understanding. In other words, works of art repay study, and these particular works of art exist here, in the present, where they are no longer the preserve of only the very rich and the very powerful. The responsibility, and the rewards, are ours.

Some words of thanks are owed. We would first like to thank Lesley Rutherford for her support throughout this project, which was first initiated before the coronavirus pandemic; her crucial advice and guidance has endured through the writing stage, much of which took place during the various lockdowns. We would also like to thank Rachel Topham for her encouragement at the proposal stage. Many friends have kindly read parts of the book and have given valuable feedback before it went to press. In some cases these have been colleagues in the teaching profession who have offered their expert advice in terms of how the book could best be geared towards use in the classroom. Our thanks go to Hatty Ekbery, Caleb Sibley, and Matt Mitchell for their words of advice and encouragement. A number of academic colleagues have also spent time reading samples of the project and their help, especially in matters of historical and theoretical detail, has been hugely valuable. We warmly thank Jon Banks, Oliver Chandler, David Curran, Sarah Moynihan, and James Savage-Hanford for their expertise. Lastly, we would like to thank Craig Lawton for sharing his specific knowledge on sources for Mahler's music.

CHRISTOPHER TARRANT AND NATALIE WILD

---

1   Carl Dahlhaus, *Foundations of Music History* (Cambridge, 1983).

Timeline of events

FROM MANNHEIM . . .

Johann Stamitz (1717–1757)
Joseph Haydn (1732–1809)

c. 1741   Johann Stamitz begins employment at the Mannheim court

Joseph Bologne, Chevalier de Saint-Georges (1745–1799)

1748   Holywell Music Room, Europe's first purpose-built concert hall,
        built in Oxford
1750   Sinfonia in D, Op. 3 No. 2 by Johann Stamitz

Wolfgang Amadeus Mozart (1756–1791)
Ludwig van Beethoven (1770–1827)

1775   Hanover Square Rooms established as the venue for subscription
            concerts in London
1778   Symphony No. 31 in D, 'Paris', by Wolfgang Amadeus Mozart
1779   Symphony No. 1 in G by Joseph Bologne, Chevalier de Saint-Georges
1789   The storming of the Bastille signals the start of the French Revolution
1795   Symphony No. 104 in D, 'London', by Joseph Haydn

Franz Schubert (1797–1828)

1800   Symphony No. 1 in C by Ludwig van Beethoven

Hector Berlioz (1803–1869)
Louise Farrenc (1804–1875)

1804   Napoleon crowns himself Emperor of the French
1805   Première of Symphony No. 3 in E♭, 'Eroica', by Ludwig van Beethoven

Felix Mendelssohn (1809–1847)
Robert Schumann (1810–1856)
Franz Liszt (1811–1886)
Richard Wagner (1813–1883)

1817   Philharmonic Society of London (now the Royal Philharmonic Society)
         commissions a new symphony by Ludwig van Beethoven
1824   Première of Symphony No. 9 in D minor, 'Choral',
         by Ludwig van Beethoven

Anton Bruckner (1824–1896)

1830   *Symphonie Fantastique* by Hector Berlioz
1831   Philharmonic Society of London commissions a new symphony
         by Felix Mendelssohn
1833   Première of Symphony No. 4 in A, 'Italian', by Felix Mendelssohn

Johannes Brahms (1833–1897)
Pyotr Ilyich Tchaikovsky (1840–1893)
Antonín Dvořák (1841–1904)

1854   Première of *Les Préludes* (the first tone poem) by Franz Liszt

Gustav Mahler (1860–1911)
Carl Nielsen (1865–1931)
Jean Sibelius (1865–1957)
Amy Beach (1867–1944)

1870   Women allowed to enrol in composition classes
         at the Paris Conservatoire
1871   Unification of Germany

Samuel Coleridge-Taylor (1875–1912)

1876   Première of Symphony No. 1 in C minor by Johannes Brahms
1893   Symphony No. 9 in E minor, 'From the New World', by Antonín Dvořák
1895   The 'Proms' begin at Queen's Hall, London
         (later moved to the Royal Albert Hall)
1896   Symphony No. 3 in D minor by Gustav Mahler (revised 1902)

. . . TO MAHLER

Case studies

Performances of all case study works included in this book can be found by following the links below.

Scores for all examples used in this book can be found on imslp.org

Chapter 2   **Sinfonia in D, Op. 3 No. 2, Johann Stamitz**
Recommended performance: Academy of Ancient Music
    (Christopher Hogwood)
bit.ly/StamitzSinfonia

Chapter 2   **Symphony No. 31 in D, 'Paris', Wolfgang Amadeus Mozart**
Recommended performance: London Mozart Players (Jane Glover)
Mvt 1 – bit.ly/MozartParis1
Mvt 2 – bit.ly/MozartParis2
Mvt 3 – bit.ly/MozartParis3

Chapter 4   **Symphony No. 4 in A, 'Italian', Felix Mendelssohn**
Recommended performance: Vienna Philharmonic Orchestra
    (Sir John Eliot Gardiner)
Mvt 1 – bit.ly/MendelssohnItalian1
Mvt 2 – bit.ly/MendelssohnItalian2
Mvt 3 – bit.ly/MendelssohnItalian3
Mvt 4 – bit.ly/MendelssohnItalian4

Chapter 6   **Symphony No. 1 in G, Joseph Bologne, Chevalier de Saint-Georges**
Recommended performance: BBC Symphony Orchestra (Rafael Payare)
bit.ly/BologneSymphony

Chapter 7   **Symphony No. 104 in D, 'London', Joseph Haydn**
Recommended performance: Vienna Philharmonic Orchestra (Bernard Haitink)
bit.ly/HaydnLondon

1
A genre in crisis?

The symphony and the 'canon'

The **symphony** is viewed traditionally as the most important genre in classical music. More than any other musical genre from the eighteenth and nineteenth centuries, the symphony – an extensive work for large ensemble – embodies the abstract ideas of music for its own sake: seriousness, transcendence, unity, even universality. This is more than can be claimed for other public genres such as **opera** with its reliance on text, or the **concerto** which hinges on the virtuosity of the soloist. This book will approach the symphony, not via the linear narrative that we are familiar with, but from a number of different perspectives: analytical, historical, and critical.

It is easy to construct a history of the symphony that only includes a handful of well-known composers, and it is even easier to write a history of the symphony that only includes male composers from the German-speaking area of Central and Northern Europe. Such histories were common during the twentieth century, and we therefore have a small group of big names that form a core repertoire (which we refer to as a **canon** of works). The vast majority of symphonies that were composed in the period 1750–1900 are invisible even to regular concert-goers, let alone the general public, and of the thousands of symphonies composed during this time, we regularly hear only a handful of them (for instance, many people have heard music by Mozart and Beethoven, but few have heard Wagenseil or Reicha). It is also important to acknowledge the extreme underrepresentation of women in the symphonic canon. This comes as a result of many complex social and economic factors. The access that most women had to a professional musical education was virtually non-existent outside the context of the opera house. Though many middle-class women received education as amateur musicians, a career as a symphonist would have been unthinkable in the eighteenth and nineteenth centuries. Even for Clara Schumann (1819–1896) and Fanny Hensel (1805–1847), two of the most successful female composers of the nineteenth century, the public genre of the symphony was out of reach.

Unlike the traditional view of the symphony as a fixed genre on a pedestal, in reality it has been constantly in flux since its development in the middle of the eighteenth century. It began as a hybrid of the Italian orchestral concerto and the opera overture, and this fusion of influences is expressed in the great diversity of works that were composed around 1750. As overtures became longer and more structurally complex, sometimes incorporating music at different contrasting tempi, there seemed to be as many different ways of writing symphonies as there were composers interested in writing them. Before conventions had been established, a definition of the symphony would have been virtually impossible.

Defining a genre

Joseph Haydn (1732–1809) is credited with laying down the standards of the symphony as we know it today – a large-scale work set in four movements for orchestra. However, this claim ignores three important points. First, it was in fact an older generation of composers including Stamitz and Sammartini who started writing works for orchestra following a multi-movement plan that Haydn would later adopt and develop. Stamitz's court orchestra in Mannheim was the original catalyst for symphonic composition in the middle of the eighteenth century, and Haydn drew significant influence from the Mannheim School for his own compositions. Secondly, Haydn's output of symphonies only stabilised in its final third (chronologically); his practice before this point was strikingly unpredictable. And thirdly, as soon as they had been established, Haydn, as much as any other composer, began to play with those conventions, often in an experimental way, frequently stretching them to the limit of audience expectations (and sometimes beyond them).

So, how do we define the symphony? Let us consider a hypothesis:

- ◆ A symphony is structured in four movements

Although this at first appears to be a basic, elementary, even banal comment, the number of exceptions to this rule starts to multiply as we begin to think about it. There are many examples from around 1800 that can be used to undermine this simple statement. Take Mozart's (1756–1791) 'Prague' Symphony, or his 'Paris' Symphony, both of which contain only three movements (both lack a Minuet). Or Beethoven's (1770–1827) Sixth Symphony, the 'Pastoral', which contains five movements (the last three of which are connected together and are performed without breaks). What about Schubert's (1797–1828) Symphony in B minor, the so-called 'Unfinished', which is constructed in only two movements (not because he died, as some people think, but because of a number of personal, compositional, and aesthetic reasons)? And we find the occasional radical exception such as Haydn's Symphony No. 60 in C major, nicknamed 'Il Distratto' ('The Distracted') which is structured in six movements.

It is easy to shoot down the claims that define a genre, yet such claims still persist. Here are some more statements about the symphony during this period, some, all, or none of which might be true. Can you think of any exceptions to these statements?

- ◆ A symphony is a piece written for orchestra
- ◆ The symphony is an example of **absolute music** (i.e., it is not influenced by non-musical ideas)
- ◆ Symphonies were written for performance in the concert hall
- ◆ Symphonies do not feature soloists
- ◆ The symphony is an Austro-German genre
- ◆ The symphony is an Italian genre
- ◆ The symphony is a European genre
- ◆ Only men wrote symphonies

- Only white Europeans wrote symphonies
- The symphony is a serious genre
- Beethoven represents the end of a tradition
- Beethoven represents the beginning of a tradition
- Berlioz wrote symphonies
- Berlioz did not write any symphonies
- A symphony can be constructed in one single movement
- Symphonies have form

As you can see, as soon as an attempt is made to describe something in terms of genre, the concrete examples escape those descriptions. This is what makes it such an exciting genre to study and explore, as well as to contribute to as a composer. Haydn certainly must have thought along these lines, for without a clear conception of what the rules of the game were, he would have found it difficult to play against them.

The 'Eroica' and the romantic turn

While the symphony may be viewed now as the most important instrumental genre in the late eighteenth century, it was not so important at the time, and certainly not as popular as the piano concerto or opera. The concerto offered the composer a chance to show off their virtuosity at the keyboard and opera was by far the more popular genre with audiences. While the opera house was a well-established institution, the purpose-built concert hall was still a new concept in the late eighteenth century, and the symphony was viewed as the type of composition that might bring you some prestige as a composer, and even some measure of fame, but rarely much money. Things began to change, however, in the first years of the nineteenth century. It was during this time that Beethoven became the pioneer of a new generation.

It is difficult to overestimate how radically Beethoven changed the essence of the symphony in the years after 1800. In his first two contributions to the genre there is a clear expansion of the materials inherited from Haydn and Mozart. These musical materials often involve pithy themes and elegantly proportioned forms; ideas of balance and closure were strongly expressed in the eighteenth-century repertoire, and even as Beethoven began to experiment with classical norms as a young composer, the eighteenth-century inheritance was audible. It is with his Third Symphony, the 'Eroica' (meaning 'heroic', composed in 1804), that we see the first instance of what the future of the genre would be. After this, the symphony would no longer be a poor relation to opera or the concerto, with composers able to produce them quickly in their hundreds. The symphony was now a major work, self-standing and serious in nature. It represented a shift away from the technical virtuosity of the star performer and towards unity and the importance of the collective effort, often having philosophical, political, or sometimes nationalistic overtones.

The symphony had expanded in length, shape, volume, and weight with Beethoven, and the ultimate radical move in his Ninth Symphony (1824) was to include a chorus and a quartet of vocal soloists in its final movement (which is as long as an entire symphony on its own). There was a feeling at this point that the genre had been stretched to such an extreme that its continued existence would be called into question. Efforts were made to follow in Beethoven's footsteps, notably by figures such as Felix Mendelssohn (1809–1847) and Robert Schumann (1810–1856), but this seemed to stall in the middle of the nineteenth century. This is not to say that there were no symphonies written at this time. Mid-nineteenth-century symphonic composition was marked by an acute crisis that was played out in the so-called 'War of the Romantics' – a series of musical and philosophical debates, exchanges, and controversies which raged around that time. On one side were those advocating for the objective purity of the genre as so-called **absolute music**. This term was originally coined by Richard Wagner (1813–1883) as an insult, but it was later self-applied by those who were advocating for it. Important figures included the academic Johannes Brahms (1833–1897) and the lawyer and philosopher Eduard Hanslick (1825–1904). On the other side of the debate stood a radical new generation of composers that included Hector Berlioz (1803–1869), Wagner, and Franz Liszt (1811–1886). Each was reimagining music by forging a new path with a distinctive voice, and all were interested in composing **programme music** (more of which in Chapter 8).

The radical changes that the symphony underwent in the middle of the nineteenth century included new possibilities such as soloists (vocal or instrumental), implied or explicit 'programmes' taken from literary or extra-musical sources, a vastly increased palette of orchestral colours and combinations, and the abandonment of a structure that had been regarded as more-or-less obligatory since Haydn. These developments were closely linked to the birth of two new genres which would jostle for position for the next hundred years. These were the **music drama** (*Gesamtkunstwerk* or 'total artwork') which Wagner had been developing as a way of bringing the different art forms (music, text, drama) together in his operas, and the **tone poem** or **symphonic poem** (*Tondichtung*) which was a piece for large orchestra, much looser in construction than the symphony, and usually taking inspiration from, if not explicitly modelled on, a literary source. Franz Liszt was its most important pioneer (examples include *Les Prèludes*, *Hamlet*, and *Prometheus*).

Centre and periphery

Vienna continued to be the centre of gravity for symphonic composition and performance during the second half of the nineteenth century, but this period is also marked by a considerable expansion of symphonic practice beyond the historical hubs of Vienna, Paris, and London, and importantly, well beyond the German-speaking world. Interestingly, it was just at the point when the perceived crisis was coming to a head that symphonic composition began to move away from Austria and Germany and take up residence in areas that have problematically been described as the European 'peripheries'. In the final quarter of the century it became normal (or perhaps even necessary) for composers in the UK, France, Denmark, Finland, Bohemia, Poland, and Russia, to name only a handful of countries, to be writing symphonies – and particularly ones that were political, patriotic, or nationalistic in tone. It was also around this time that such far-flung places as Copenhagen, Helsinki, and St Petersburg were developing as important concert-giving cities.

The concept of centre and periphery makes the figure of Gustav Mahler (1860–1911) particularly intriguing. Mahler was active as a composer from the 1880s until his death in 1911.

On paper he has all the markings of an Austro-German canonical composer in the romantic tradition: he lived and worked in Vienna, his music is now considered part of the core repertoire and he wrote nine (which, for some reason, is a magical number for composers) symphonies. As soon as we peer beneath the surface, however, we find a much more complex relationship with tradition. Although he worked in the undisputed epicentre of symphonic composition, he came from Moravia, which lies in the modern-day Czech Republic, but which in Mahler's time formed part of the vast Austro-Hungarian Empire. Although by no means a backwater, it was not a major cosmopolitan centre. During his time in Vienna he was considered something of an outsider, not just because of his Bohemian heritage but crucially because of his Jewish faith, which meant he was subject to various restrictions imposed by the Viennese musical establishment.

Mahler was not a composer by trade. Rather, he made his living on the conducting podium and spent his summers, when he was not required to conduct opera, in the country working on his vast symphonies. Many of these works, which are now widely considered to be timeless masterworks, were met with scant praise at the time they were first performed. It took the efforts of musicians, conductors, and scholars decades later to promote and, to a certain degree, rehabilitate his output. The most important figures in this effort were the conductor Leonard Bernstein (1918–1990) and the philosopher Theodor Adorno (1903–1969). There is also an aesthetic argument to be made: although superficially we might consider Mahler's music to be a contributor to romanticism (however that may be described musically: big tunes, lush orchestration, dramatic tension), digging deeper, it becomes apparent that there are some strikingly un-romantic and often overtly modernist ideas that can be found in his output, and that it may be more advantageous to consider Mahler as belonging to the beginning of the twentieth century rather than as a residue of the nineteenth.

Historical problems

The paragraphs above are not intended to provide a complete picture of the history of the symphony over 150 years. Rather, they are an attempt to challenge, question, and probe conventional ideas, including that the symphony is somehow 'core' or privileged over and above other forms of composition, or that the history of symphonic composition unfolds in a straightforwardly linear fashion. Addressing the second point, the fact that Hector Berlioz's radical and at times monstrous *Symphonie Fantastique* (1830) was composed before Mendelssohn's much more classically conservative 'Italian' Symphony (1833), and that both symphonies retain their place in the established and timeless concert repertoire, should arguably give us enough cause to abandon any idea of a linear progression from classicism to romanticism and then to modernism (whatever those words might mean in practice). Regarding the symphony as the core of the concert repertoire, these works were not easily accessible at the time of composition to anybody who wanted to listen – quite the contrary. The vast majority of the sort of notated compositions that we understand to belong to the Western Art Music tradition (one in which the musical conception is notated and then reproduced in sound in a performance) would have been heard in churches – not venues where symphonies would have been regularly performed. It is therefore all the more remarkable that the symphony has survived.

Such a sense of survival is not just a surprise in economic terms (after all, paying for large numbers of musicians can be expensive); it is also striking on purely aesthetic grounds. This became particularly noticeable after Beethoven's Ninth Symphony (first performed in 1824). It is remarkable that anyone could compose a symphony after such an existential threat to the identity of the genre, and critics at the time had declared that the genre was now dead. This was a mantra that was repeated throughout the nineteenth century: someone writes a symphony that seems to kill the genre stone dead, as if to say 'the symphony is done – THE END', only for someone else to come along and write another one. There are few better examples of this than Pyotr Ilyich Tchaikovsky's (1840–1893) Sixth Symphony in B minor, 'Pathétique', Op. 74, which ends with a slow finale that descends to the bowels of the orchestra in a morbid farewell (the composer died less than a fortnight after the première). Yet this was followed only a matter of months later in spring 1894 by the first performance of Carl Nielsen's (1865–1931) First Symphony – a work with a youthful disregard for conventions of tonality, form, and scoring, and which belongs to the output of a new and younger generation of early-modernist symphonists. In many respects, the history of the symphony in this period is a history, against the odds, of its survival.

The structure of the book

This book aims to provide a starting point for those who are interested in the symphony from a pedagogical position, for students, as well as for those who may simply be interested in learning more about the music they hear on a regular basis. It is divided into three parts, each of which has a distinct aim. Part I establishes some of the main contexts for symphonic composition. Who was composing these things? What were the criteria that regulated the genre? Where were these compositions performed? Who was performing them? And who was paying for it? Part II deals with the material detail of the symphony during the period in question. These works, which are perceptible to us through the trace they leave in their scores, exist not only in history but also now in the present, and as musicians we have a responsibility to engage with them independently of what others may have said. Therefore, the central section of the book aims analytically to deepen our engagement with individual works as well as the genre more broadly. Topics covered include the small-scale structure of the music – individual themes and motives (broadly referred to as musical *syntax*); the large-scale organisation and combination of these smaller components (which we usually consider in terms of musical *form*); and closely linked to both of these, the question of how *tonality* operates in the period under discussion. After this excavation of the musical detail, Part III turns to broader questions of genre. What makes a symphony? What might ideas such as politics, nationality, and nationalism have to do with symphonic composition during this time?

The structure of this book is neither chronological (though there is a sense of this) nor composer-centred, but rather it is organised thematically. It cycles through the various topics as they relate to the whole 150-year period under discussion with the aim of repeatedly revisiting composers, events, and ideas, each time from a new and different perspective. The structure builds up a series of interlaced layers, with each chapter deepening and enriching the others. During this process the book will focus in on important milestones, touchpoints, case studies, events, works, and composers as they serve to exemplify the debates and controversies surrounding the genre. This generates a deeper and more engaging narrative than can be provided by a linear historical account. The book has been written to be enjoyed from cover to cover, but it might also be employed in a more piecemeal fashion; readers may wish to dip in and out, reading certain sections as the need arises. Prior knowledge of the genre is not a prerequisite for a fruitful engagement with the debates and materials contained here, and, although the ability to engage with notated scores is necessary to fully grasp the ideas presented in Part II, the majority of the book will be accessible to anyone who is interested in listening to this music and learning more about it.

Part I: Contexts

2
The early symphony

Eighteenth-century music and the figure of the *Kapellmeister*

For eighteenth-century composers the role of **Kapellmeister** (master of the chapel choir) at a wealthy court was a desirable position to hold. The scope of the job stretched beyond simply composing music for the court orchestra. Other duties the *Kapellmeister* would have been expected to undertake included rehearsing, conducting, administrative tasks, and teaching members of the household and other wealthy courtiers. It is therefore useful to think of this role as something similar to a civil servant who could produce new works at speed, in step with fast-changing musical fashions, and for immediate use. The more familiar idea of the composer as a romantic artist concerned with carefully shaping masterpieces for future generations had not yet emerged and would not fully materialise until the nineteenth century. Some households, such as those at Esterházy and Mannheim, allowed the *Kapellmeister* great creative freedom and access to some of the best musicians in Europe. These circumstances shaped the development of the symphony; the music that resulted from these employments, aided by advances in printed music and the establishment of dedicated publishing houses, spread to places such as London, Paris, and Leipzig.

The origins of the symphony

In the seventeenth century, instrumental music was most commonly used for interludes at the theatre or in vocal works such as operas, motets, cantatas, and oratorios. In particular, the Italian **sinfonia** played an important role in setting the mood and creating a sense of anticipation at the start of an opera, similar to an overture, before the vocal numbers communicated the drama more directly through their text. Alessandro Scarlatti (1660–1725) was a key figure who pioneered this genre. By the beginning of the eighteenth century these instrumental interludes had been expanded and developed, and they were constructed within a set of recognisable formal and tonal conventions. Binary-form movements became standard practice. A slow rate of harmonic change, a more cadence-orientated musical language, and a sharper sense of tonal tension (using primary harmonic colours and dispensing with the baroque preference for harmonic complexity), combined with the increased use of flashy displays of texture and orchestration heightened the drama and dynamism of this repertoire. Around the same time there were also three different types of concerto at play, particularly among instrumental composers in the Lombardy region of Northern Italy: the **concerto grosso** (a small *concertino* ensemble of solo instruments playing against a larger ensemble named the *ripieno*);

the **orchestral concerto** (a work for solo instrument accompanied by a large ensemble); and perhaps most significantly the **ripieno concerto** (an ensemble work with no real distinction between solo and tutti passages). Many of these different works followed a three-movement (fast–slow–fast) structure.

Other influences on what would become the concert symphony from the musical centre of northern Italy included the **sonata da camera**, or chamber sonata, which was a series of dances, the **sonata di chiesa**, or church sonata, which comprised a series of abstract move-ments written to suit the religious setting, and the **trio sonata**, written for two treble instru-ments and basso continuo. As well as being a hub of activity for composers, northern Italy (especially Cremona) also became the centre of great master violin makers such as Nicolò Amati (1596–1684), Antonio Stradivari (1644–1737), and Giuseppe Guarneri (1698–1744), all of whom produced instruments that have never since been surpassed in quality of sound. The rapidly developing repertoire of instrumental music created a demand for great instruments, and these workshops were able to provide them in their hundreds.

Early developments: Sammartini and the Milanese school

Three significant schools of symphonic writing emerged during the 1730s. These were the Milanese school, known for the music of G. B. Sammartini, the Viennese school, with sym-phonic works by G. C. Wagenseil, and the Mannheim school, led by J. Stamitz. It is the Milanese school and the Mannheim school that we turn our attention to first.

The **Milanese school** was one of the first symphonic schools in Europe. The most sig-nificant of its composers was Giovanni Battista Sammartini (c. 1700–1775), who was *maestro di capella* of the ducal chapel in Milan. As well as writing opera overtures, Sammartini wrote in excess of 70 'concert symphonies', which were unlike the dramatic overtures of the opera house and the serious symphonies of the church. These works demonstrate more substantial thematic development than the Italian overture, while cultivating a more lyrical, melody-led texture, much more like the ripieno concerto and the trio sonata. The vast majority of these are scored for strings only. They are mostly in three movements and demonstrate the elegance and grace of what would later be described as the **galant** style (see below).

The emergence of **sonata form** is detectable in much of Sammartini's symphonic writing. In the first movement of his Symphony in F major, for example, the material heard in the dom-inant in the first half – the secondary theme – is repeated in the tonic in the second half. The return of previously off-tonic music in the tonic towards the end of the piece became one of the defining strategies of large-scale musical construction in the middle of the century, although it would be decades before the classical approach of a full recapitulation of all the material would become normal (see Chapter 6).

Johann Stamitz and the Mannheim school

Owing to the popularity of works by composers such as Sammartini, Jommelli, Galuppi, Monn, and Wagenseil, the symphony as a genre spread north across Europe. The court of the Elector Palatine at Mannheim Palace in south-west Germany was a crucial centre of compositional activity, led by the Bohemian violinist and composer Johann Stamitz (1717–1757). In the early 1740s Elector Charles Philip III appointed Johann Stamitz as the director of court music. The Mannheim court had a reputation for recruiting the finest musicians, and its orchestra was the envy of many other composers. Mozart and Haydn would both visit Mannheim at different points to hear the music for themselves, and Mozart even trialled his own symphonies with the orchestra. Stamitz stayed there for around fifteen years, during which time he wrote many symphonies and works for chamber ensembles.

Influenced by the Italian opera overtures, and particularly those of Jommelli, Stamitz and his contemporaries at Mannheim expanded the binary structures into much larger proportions. This expansion required more tonal stability, which in turn required a slower rate of harmonic change. This sharply contrasts with the rapidly changing and heavily ornamented baroque textures of early eighteenth-century instrumental music. In order to avoid a slowing down of energy that might result from this, Stamitz experimented with rhythmic and textural devices that helped to create momentum and drive. These effects would later be assimilated into the canon of symphonic music and include the **Mannheim Walze** ('roller'), **Mannheim hammer strokes**, sighs, and the **Mannheim *crescendo***. As well as dynamic effects, his symphonies demonstrate an extension of phrase lengths, a greater focus on thematic development, and more contrast of material within movements. In fact, it is possible to produce a sort of 'blueprint' for a Mannheim symphony, demonstrating where within the structure these different effects and characteristics can be found.

CASE STUDY: SINFONIA IN D, OP. 3 NO. 2 (1750) BY JOHANN STAMITZ

Let's consider this early four-movement symphony written in 1750. In the middle of the eighteenth century it became increasingly common for composers to follow the **sinfonia a 8** configuration of strings (violin I, violin II, viola, basso continuo), two oboes, and two horns. With the musicians employed at Mannheim, Stamitz was able to expand this even further to include trumpets and timpani, as seen in this particular example.

First, there would often be an energetic 'call to attention' statement to emphasise the tonic. In the Sinfonia in D, it takes the form of hammer strokes in groups of three (see **EX. 2.1** bars 1–4). After the initial statement we find a Mannheim 'roller' – a *tutti crescendo* with a rising melody over a pedal point that builds tension up to a release of energy (see **EX. 2.1** bars 5–13). Similar to Sammartini, Stamitz made use of simple, diatonic melodies showcasing lyrical, graceful ideas to provide a change of mood. This is particularly evident in the secondary theme (see **EX. 2.2**).

The widespread influence of the Mannheim symphonies, especially those of Stamitz, justify its importance as the centre of the development of the genre. It is important to note, however, that all of these effects originated before Stamitz came to prominence, particularly in the operatic overtures of Jommelli. Even the 'roller', which became the signature of Mannheim symphonists, was a common gesture in overtures as a way of building energy. It was the sheer number of symphonies that came out of the Mannheim court around the middle of the eighteenth century that generated its reputation as the crucible of symphonic writing. It is in the scoring and orchestration, however, that the Mannheim symphonies overtake the Italian

EX. 2.1 HAMMER STROKES AND MANNHEIM ROLLER IN STAMITZ, SINFONIA IN D, OP. 3 NO. 2, I, BARS 1–13

EX. 2.2 LYRICAL SECOND THEME IN STAMITZ, SINFONIA IN D, OP. 3 NO. 2, I, BARS 37–44

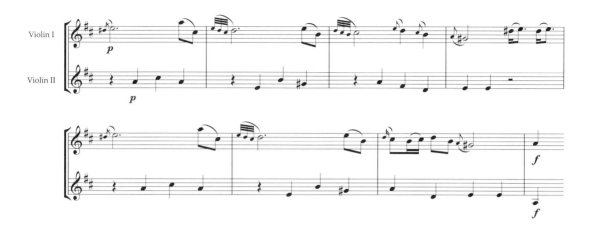

models, particularly in their use of solo passages for woodwind and horns. This is all evident in the same work. The second movement, a lilting Andantino in the subdominant key of G major, gives independent lines to the woodwind while the strings accompany.

EX. 2.3 STAMITZ, SINFONIA IN D, OP. 3 NO. 2, II, BARS 14–20

Despite his reputation as the 'Father of the Symphony', Haydn was not the first symphonist to include a Minuet and Trio as a third movement. Composers of the Viennese school, including Gassmann, Hofmann, and Dittersdorf, had experimented with a four-movement structure of fast–slow–Minuet–fast in the 1760s, but Stamitz was already doing this as early as the 1740s. Most of the symphonies that came from Mannheim followed this pattern, albeit with the Minuet often being a short incidental movement without the more developed, contrasting trios of later classical symphonies by Haydn, Mozart, and Beethoven.

The assimilation of these Mannheim characteristics into the symphonic output of the eighteenth century (and beyond) happened as a result of several events. First, the reputation of the court orchestra drew attention across Europe and attracted travelling composers including Mozart, who journeyed to Mannheim in 1777 in search of employment. The orchestra was significantly larger than any in Austria, and included trumpets, timpani, and even clarinets. The German writer Daniel Schubart wrote about its dynamic power in pictorial terms:

> No orchestra in the world has ever surpassed that of the Mannheim in performance. Its *forte* is like thunder, its *crescendo* a cataract, its *diminuendo* a crystal stream bubbling into the distance, its *piano* a breath of spring. The winds are all used just as they should be: they lift and support, or fill out and animate, the storm of the violins.[1]

Secondly, unlike the Italian and Austrian tradition of salon concerts reserved for the wealthy upper class, music at Mannheim was composed for twice-weekly public concerts that were free of charge. This undoubtedly fuelled the unrivalled reputation of Mannheim as a musical hub. Thirdly, in the mid-eighteenth century, publishing houses responded to public tastes for music by foreign composers by offering collections of six symphonies that included those of composers from the Mannheim court. Another composer from Mannheim, Franz Xaver Richter (1709–1789), had six of his symphonies published in London after a visit to England in 1754. All of these factors helped the spread of the symphony as a popular genre among audiences and composers, and it is possible to hear the influence of the Mannheim school in some of the genre's most important works:

- A key work from the symphonic canon, **Beethoven's Symphony No. 3 in E♭, 'Eroica'**, opens with hammer strokes calling the audience to attention before the primary theme begins (see **EX. 2.4**).
- **Mozart**, who eagerly – yet ultimately unsuccessfully – pursued employment at Mannheim, uses a 'roller' near the start of his **Symphony No. 5 in B♭ major (K.22)**. This music was composed when Mozart was a child, long before his visit to Mannheim, which shows how pervasive the technique was by the 1760s (see **EX. 2.5**).
- The exploitation of dynamic contrast and sudden accents for which the Mannheim school was so well known is the vehicle for increased dramatic intensity in the second movement of **Haydn's 'Surprise' Symphony, No. 94 in G major**. Here, Haydn takes the basic idea of a loud chord and turns it into the subject of a whole variation in which every bar has a loud chord (see **EX. 2.6A** and its variation **EX. 2.6B**).

---

1   C.F.D. Schubart, *Ideen zu einer Äesthetik der Tonkunst*, ed. Ludwig Schubart (Vienna: J. V. Dergen, 1806, repr. Leipzig: Reclam, 1977), 118–119.

Developments in instrumentation

There was no standard combination of instruments in the eighteenth-century symphony. The string section remained a constant, but pairs of woodwind and brass instruments were added in various combinations depending on what players were available. The sinfonia a 8 format (2 oboes, 2 horns, and strings) remained common until the 1770s. Sometimes the wind parts would be interchangeable depending on what musicians the *Kapellmeister* had at their disposal. It was not unusual in the mid-eighteenth century for court oboists to double on clarinets, and the orchestra at Mannheim was one of the first to employ them as early as 1759. Clarinets are usually considered the latecomers to the symphony orchestra – Haydn did not use them until the 1790s – but they can be found in several of Stamitz's symphonies from this time.[2] When these works were later published in Paris, the title page stipulated that clarinets were preferable, but could be replaced by oboes, flutes, or violins.[3]

2   Colin Lawson, *Mozart Clarinet Concerto* (Cambridge: Cambridge University Press, 1996), 9.

3   Lawson, *Mozart Clarinet Concerto*, 7.

EX. 2.4 HAMMER STROKES IN BEETHOVEN, SYMPHONY NO. 3 IN E♭, 'EROICA', I, BARS 1–8

EX. 2.6A SUDDEN ACCENTS IN HAYDN, 'SURPRISE' SYMPHONY NO. 94 IN G, II, BARS 1–16

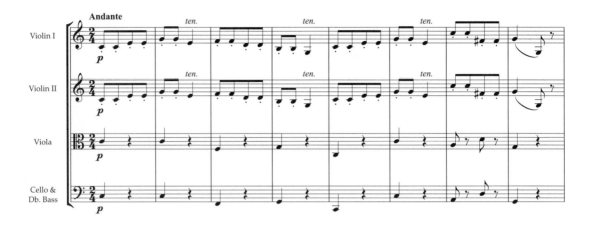

CASE STUDY: SYMPHONY NO. 31 IN D, 'PARIS' (1778) BY WOLFGANG AMADEUS MOZART

The influence the Mannheim orchestra had on Mozart is clear in his 'Paris' Symphony. After writing the symphony, and clearly quite taken with the new sounds the clarinets offered, he wrote to his father: '[a]h, if only we had clarinets too! You cannot imagine the glorious effect of a symphony with flutes, oboes, and clarinets.'[4] The effect of this more fulsome orchestration – with pairs of flutes, oboes, clarinets, bassoons, horns, and trumpets as well as timpani and strings – would become the norm in the nineteenth century, but by eighteenth-century standards it was extraordinary: compare Mozart's Symphony No. 29 in A, which asks only for strings, horns, and oboes, with the much larger orchestra of the 'Paris' Symphony. The full woodwind choir is used throughout, allowing Mozart to experiment with combinations and timbres within an otherwise tried-and-tested format for Parisian audiences. Whereas Stamitz and Haydn typically reserved clarinets for reinforcing the louder passages, Mozart's 'Paris' Symphony allowed them a far more prominent role.

In the secondary theme of the first movement, for example, the clarinets (along with bassoons) respond to the idea presented by the upper strings (EX. 2.7).

---

4   All letters reproduced from the translations in Emily Anderson, *The Letters of Mozart and His Family*, II (2nd edn, New York: St. Martin's, 1966).

EX. 2.7 MOZART, 'PARIS' SYMPHONY, I, BARS 53–58

In the recapitulation, the clarinets join the violas in the ascending scale (bar 180; bar 184).

EX. 2.8 MOZART, 'PARIS' SYMPHONY, I, BARS 180–186

In both examples, the lighter texture allows for the distinctive clarinet sound to be heard. The influence of the Mannheim orchestra is found in the combinations of clarinets and bassoons, horns and oboes, and flutes and oboes, and is evident from the opening hammer strokes swiftly followed by a Mannheim 'rocket' (an ascending, accelerating scale) (**EX. 2.9**).

Towards the end of the movement, a Mannheim crescendo is added to the closing material (bars 247–251, and again in bars 266–270).

EX. 2.10 MOZART, 'PARIS' SYMPHONY, I, BARS 247–251

It was not until he moved to Vienna in 1781 that Mozart could again include clarinets in his music, as there was none at his disposal in Salzburg. His final offerings in the genre, a series of three symphonies – No. 39 in E♭ major, No. 40 in G minor, and No. 41, the 'Jupiter' Symphony in C major – were composed within a three-month period in the summer of 1788. They appear to have been written in response to Haydn's six 'Paris' Symphonies of 1785–6. Symphony No. 39 in E♭ replaces the oboes with clarinets, and Symphony No. 40 in G minor has two versions, with added clarinets in Mozart's later revision. The 'Jupiter' Symphony is more conventional in its scoring, using only bassoons, oboes and a single flute in its woodwind choir.

Classical 'topics'

The classical symphonic style is different from earlier orchestral music because of the abundance of different themes and moods ('topics') that can be combined and juxtaposed. The norm for the earlier part of the eighteenth century would have been for the composer to choose a single mood or sentiment and develop it over the course of the piece. In the later part of the century a wider palette of colours was quickly becoming available and composers were beginning to combine them in exciting ways. These 'topics' include identifiable moods or flavours which would have been recognisable to eighteenth-century audiences. Some of the most commonly used classical topics are:

- **Fanfare** – using the natural harmonics of the horns and trumpets, the fanfare topic is one of the easiest to identify. Sometimes fanfares use triplet or other characteristic rhythms and triadic melodies, and they are positioned strategically either to announce something new or to conclude or celebrate a goal that has just been achieved.

- **Singing style** – a melody that imitates the singing voice. This could be played by the violins or by a solo woodwind instrument such as an oboe or a clarinet.

- **Military** – imitating a military band. Prominent use of trumpets and timpani combined with dotted rhythms is the usual approach, and this can be supplemented with other percussion (such as side drum) and flute or piccolo, which can imitate the sound of the military fife – see Haydn's 'Military' Symphony, No. 100 in G major.

- *Stile antico* – 'antique style'. This is signalled by the use of 'white notes' – minims and semibreves – and lots of polyphonic lines, making the music look (and sound) like the type of polyphony associated with earlier sacred styles from the renaissance. Sometimes this would involve the use of a *cantus firmus* – a short melodic idea in long notes – around which some faster contrapuntal activity could be arranged. The finale of Mozart's Symphony No. 41 features a clear example of this topic right at the beginning.

- **Pastoral** – summoning images of nature, the countryside, and rural life. F major is the traditional key for this topic, though D major was also used. There are lots of indicators of the pastoral topic, including gently lilting themes evoking the rural landscape, prominent use of pastoral instruments such as oboes (evoking the image of the shepherd with his pipe), horns (associated with hunting), and violas (associated with folk music), and the suggestion of peasant songs and dances. Beethoven's Sixth Symphony in F major is the central example of this sort of music.

- **Minuet**, **Waltz**, **March** – all sorts of formal dances could be invoked easily by using the appropriate combinations of tempo and metre.

Clear examples of the juxtaposition of topics abound in **Mozart's 'Jupiter' Symphony**, which stages a continued struggle between a normative symphonic style with its military associations signalled by prominent use of trumpets and timpani, and the somewhat more reflective 'singing style' and *stile antico* topics. Even within the first few bars of the symphony we can hear the opposition of the militaristic and heavily scored Mannheim hammer strokes alternating with the more lyrical *cantabile* figures in the violins.

EX. 2.11   MOZART, SYMPHONY NO. 41 IN C, 'JUPITER', I, BARS 1–4

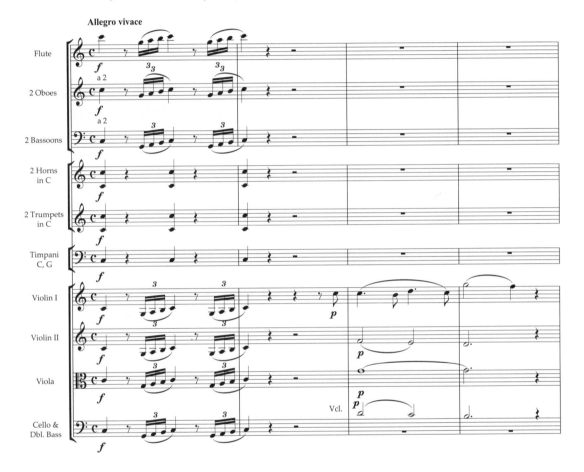

This juxtaposition is intensified in the finale, which begins quietly with the *stile antico* topic, summoning the idea of the ancient sacred style. Somewhat like a piece of plainchant, the melody is set in semibreves and is subject to devices such as imitation and especially imitative polyphony. This is set against a more raucous and rhythmically active symphonic texture, giving the impression of a struggle between the two styles. The movement's coda finally saturates the *stile antico* topic by setting the plainchant theme against four other themes from the movement *at the same time*, as a double fugue (see **EX. 2.11**). Eventually the military–symphonic texture engulfs the plainchant theme, winning out and ending the work in triumphal fashion.

EX. 2.12 MOZART, 'JUPITER' SYMPHONY, IV, BARS 373–403 (CODA)

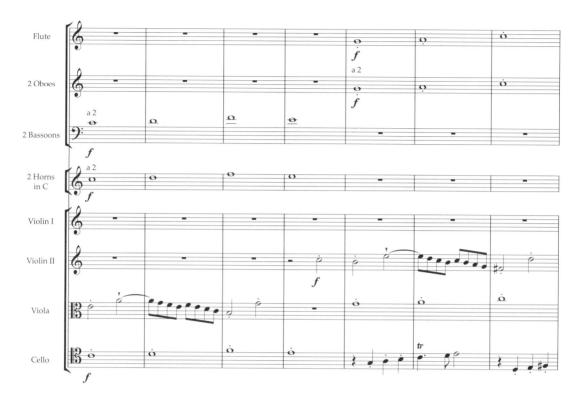

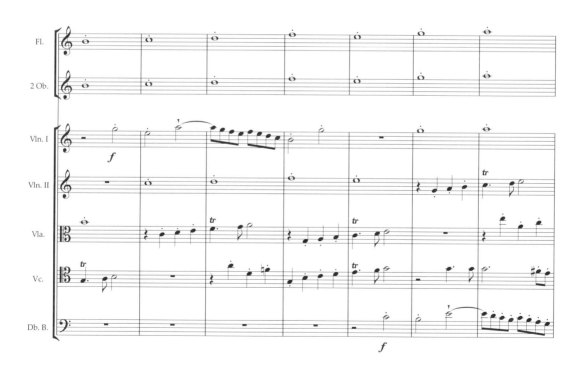

Sturm und Drang (storm and stress) was an important minor-mode topic that was used by Haydn, Mozart, and others to express turbulent, unstable, or stormy ideas. Mozart's two G minor symphonies, Nos 25 and 40, fall into this category, and many examples come from the middle-period Haydn, with his 'Farewell' Symphony, No. 45 in F♯ minor being a clear example. Symphonies in minor keys were quite rare in the eighteenth century. They only account for about two percent of all symphonies written in the age of Haydn and Mozart but became much more popular in the nineteenth century.[5] Among the things that set the *Sturm und Drang* mood apart from other classical topics is the regular use of the so-called 'minor-key pathotype' – a collection of pitches which could be used in various iterations to create thematic content. These pitches were the tonic, dominant, flattened sixth, and leading note, and they were most frequently ordered in a way that accentuates the falling diminished seventh (see **FIG. 2.1**). One way of understanding this is to think of the tonic and dominant notes as outlining the minor tonic triad and the other two notes outlining a diminished seventh, a semitone either side of the triad, 'stretching' it out, and perhaps therefore 'stressing' it out![6]

FIG. 2.1 THE MINOR-KEY PATHOTYPE

Galant style

Music that was composed for the entertainment of the leisured classes in the eighteenth century tended to rely on a collection of patterns that were commonly available. Many of these musical patterns, or 'schemata', originated in the Italian courts during the seventeenth century, but they quickly began to gain currency across northern Europe. This mode of composition eventually coalesced into what we now call the 'galant style'. Galant music can be found in lots of genres. It is regularly found in baroque opera and the trio sonata in the early part of the eighteenth century, but it also became an established mode of sonata, quartet, and symphonic composition. Therefore, we can say that the galant style is embedded in music of both the late baroque and classical periods.

It might seem odd simply to take something that already exists and incorporate it into your own music. For a long time it has been common to approach eighteenth-century music with a nineteenth-century attitude towards creativity. Since around Beethoven's time, to compose meant to invent new musical material. During the eighteenth century, however, composition was largely an art of combination (*ars combinatoria*) in which the graceful, elegant, and engaging arrangement of *typical* musical figures was prized above the invention of *original* ones. Although this may seem strange – inventing new music is what composers do, by modern standards – it might be helpful to think of the eighteenth-century *Kapellmeister* as achieving something similar

5   Matthew Riley, *The Viennese Minor-Key Symphony in the Age of Haydn and Mozart* (Oxford: Oxford University Press, 2014), 1.

6   James Hepokoski, *A Sonata Theory Handbook* (New York: Oxford University Press USA, 2021), 138–140.

to a skilled chef who serves a meal by combining dishes from a menu, or perhaps an ice skater who executes a set of recognised 'figures' which they have combined into a routine.[7] One of the outcomes of this strategy was that it became feasible to produce large quantities of high-quality music in a short space of time. Rather like building a wall, it's a lot quicker if you don't have to design and make each brick as you go! In this environment it was absolutely possible for talented children to compose sonatas, quartets, and even symphonies – a phenomenon that went into decline after 1800 (with the important exception of Mendelssohn).[8]

Let's look at an example. The first section of **Mozart's Symphony No. 13 in F, K.112**, is constructed from a set of 15 musical events – schemata – which are outlined in **FIG. 2.2.** The score is shown in **EX. 2.13**. There is barely a note in this music that does not belong to one of

FIG. 2.2 *GALANT SCHEMATA* FROM MOZART'S SYMPHONY NO. 13 IN F, K.112

7   Robert O. Gjerdingen uses this exact analogy in *Music in the Galant Style* (New York: Oxford University Press USA, 2007), 7.
8   Gjerdingen, *Music in the Galant Style*.

the commonly available schemata. The allure of this music, though, is not in the way Mozart 'invented' his materials, but in how they have been creatively combined, ordered, deployed, and decorated. You may wish to have a go at playing the basic shapes at the keyboard (or fretboard) to get used to them before listening to a recording of the symphony – some of the patterns that the 15-year-old Mozart used might be familiar, others less so. This music gives a good demonstration of how the galant schemata were used in the 1770s. It's also interesting to see how the idea of classical balance and symmetry is expressed in this excerpt, which begins with a triadic descent followed by the quiescenza schema (a tonic pedal over which the upper voices outline chords I, IV, V, and I) and closes with a quiescenza followed by a triadic ascent. These sorts of symmetries and framing effects were quite common in the eighteenth century. If you would like to investigate these ideas further, Robert O. Gjerdingen's *Music in the Galant Style* is the authoritative book on the topic.[9]

◆   ◆   ◆

Now that we have addressed some of the key features of the symphony as it emerged from the older genres of the concerto and the overture, it is important to have a deeper understanding of some of the institutional structures that helped to shape its development in the classical period and into the nineteenth century. Many of these institutions had already existed in southern Europe (such as the musical conservatory), which then spread north to foster symphonic music. Others were new inventions, such as concert halls and philharmonic societies. These nineteenth-century institutions played a fundamental role in the way music was taught, composed, disseminated, and performed, and they continue to shape the way we hear and play music today.

9   Robert O. Gjerdingen, *Music in the Galant Style* (New York: Oxford University Press USA, 2007).

3
Patronage and public concerts

In the mid-eighteenth century, being a composer was not normally a freelance job. The main employers of composers during this time were the church and the aristocracy. **Patronage** describes this transaction; composers were given a salary and access to court musicians by aristocratic benefactors who were keen to maintain a busy cultural life at court. The aristocracy needed to project prosperity in order to sustain their power, and music-making at court was an important vehicle for doing this while impressing allies and rivals. Mozart and Haydn were first and foremost performing musicians before they were composers, and their reputation as virtuoso performers led to them being employed at wealthy courts across Europe. In Haydn's case, this meant a lengthy career working for a single court. For Mozart, it meant a string of much shorter engagements that led to a lot of travelling. This chapter will consider the impact of private patrons on classical composers such as Haydn, Mozart, and Beethoven, and explore how the emerging middle classes and their tastes for public concerts shaped the careers of freelance composers in the nineteenth century. This in turn changed the wider public's appetite for the symphony from relatively small, concise works composed for just a few performances to a far more substantial art form with a long shelf life. We will also consider the emergence of the concert hall as an important venue for performances of large orchestral works, and the rise of philharmonic societies and subscription concerts.

Haydn in Eisenstadt and London

Haydn was fortunate that he was invited to work for one of the most noble and wealthy families in Europe, the Esterházys in Eisenstadt, within the Austro-Hungarian Empire. He was promoted to *Kapellmeister* in 1766, which gave him the musical freedom to experiment with new instrumental combinations, and access to the high quality of musicians and facilities that the court boasted. Haydn's early symphonies demonstrate that he was able to rely on virtuosic abilities in his woodwind and brass players, and even double bass players, as evidenced by the solo part in the trio of the third movement of his Sixth Symphony, 'Le Matin'. In fact, his letters reveal that he was given a large degree of musical autonomy at court, even though he didn't at first enjoy much personal freedom. In a conversation with his biographer, Haydn commented that '[a]s head of an orchestra I was able to make experiments, observe what makes a [good] effect and what weakens it, and thus revise, expand, cut, take chances;

I was cut off from the world, nobody around me could upset my self-confidence, and so I had to become original.'[1]

Haydn's employer, Prince Nicolaus, had a voracious musical appetite, and the symphony was the perfect way to satisfy it. Haydn was able to demonstrate the abilities of the orchestra, and to experiment with different sounds, forms, and combinations, all ensuring his output remained fresh and inventive. A perfect example of this is in his 'Farewell' Symphony, composed in 1772. During the summer months, the court moved away from Eisenstadt to the Palace of Esterháza in modern-day Hungary, meaning that musicians were separated from their families for several months. To demonstrate the consternation of the employees, Haydn composed this symphony in the unorthodox key of F♯ minor, a key usually reserved for particularly anguished emotional states (see also the F♯ minor slow movement of Mozart's Piano Concerto No. 23 in A, K.488). This also meant that bespoke crooks for the French horns had to be custom made (horns in F♯ were not normally available). Haydn composed the final movement, an Adagio, as a sort of musical protest. As the movement draws to an end, the players finish and are instructed to leave the stage one by one, putting out their candles as they do so, until there are just two violinists left playing *pianissimo*. The music served its purpose, and the court musicians were granted leave to return home to their families at Eisenstadt.

In the 1780s, Haydn's output focused on instrumental works such as quartets and keyboard sonatas, as well as works for the theatre, but in the latter part of the eighteenth century he was able to secure significant commissions from external public patrons. In 1785, one Chevalier de Saint-Georges (1745–1799) (whose First Symphony we will explore in Chapter 6) was charged with arranging a commission of six symphonies from Haydn for the newly named *Concert de la Loge Olympique* concert series in Paris. Saint-Georges conducted the première performances of the six 'Paris' symphonies (Nos. 82–87) to great acclaim, prompting particular praise from Queen Marie Antoinette. Haydn's reputation as a symphonic composer was bolstered, and he received more invitations for commissioned works.

When Paul Anton II assumed the title at Esterházy in 1790, he disbanded the orchestra and opera group. However, Haydn continued to be employed by the family, allowing him to travel across Europe as a composer but with the security of a regular income, and with his name still associated with the Esterházy family. This meant that he was able to return to Vienna as a freelance composer. His reputation strengthened by the publication of his music, Haydn attracted the attention of the violinist and concert promoter Joseph Salomon, who invited the composer to London to contribute to his 1790–1 and 1794–5 concert series. Salomon commissioned 12 symphonies that would later become known as the 'London' Symphonies. Among them was the 'Military' Symphony, No. 100 – a work with military-style influences that appealed to audiences' tastes in England, which was at war with France at that time. In a 1795 concert his 'London' Symphony, No. 104, was premièred to an enthusiastic audience at the King's Theatre. It was an instant success with its memorable, playful material, use of dynamic contrasts and unexpected rests. Although still technically under the private patronage of the Esterházy family, Haydn had managed to make a name for himself outside of the palace, facilitating a move towards more public commissions from wealthy patrons.

1   James Webster, 'Haydn's Aesthetics' in Caryl Clark, ed., *The Cambridge Companion to Haydn* (Cambridge: Cambridge University Press, 2005), 30–44.

Mozart in Vienna and Europe

In contrast to Haydn's time at Eisenstadt, it was customary for musicians who were not employed at court to travel from city to city to perform for various aristocratic families. Wolfgang
Amadeus Mozart was used to this lifestyle, having toured Europe with his sister and father,
performing for wealthy households since he was a boy. In 1777, Mozart requested that he be
relieved of his duties at the small court at Salzburg, and for the first time he was free to tour
without his father. On his travels he spent more than four months at Mannheim, where the
young Mozart befriended the court musicians and tried (unsuccessfully) to secure a post.

　As part of his work as a touring composer, he visited Paris. Mozart's Symphony No. 31
in D major (1778), now known as his 'Paris' Symphony, was first performed at the *Concert
Spirituel* – one of Europe's first public concert series. The composer was there to seek a court
position, but no such offer of employment was given. Instead, Mozart sought a commission
from one of the best orchestras in France at the time, that of the *Concert Spirituel*. In order
for this new work to be a success, it had to cater to the musical tastes of the Parisian audience.
Though scathing of the intellect of audience members in the French capital, Mozart knew how
to please them. Of the opening of the symphony, he wrote 'I have been careful not to neglect
le premier coup d'archet [a tutti entrance at the very start of a symphony with all string players
playing on a down bow] – and that is quite sufficient [to make a symphony successful in Paris].
What a fuss the oxen here make of this trick! The devil take me if I can see any difference! They
all begin together, just as they do in other places.'[2] In this respect, the *coup d'archet* that begins
the 'Paris' Symphony is almost foolproof.

　Further evidence of his attempts to achieve success with this symphony can be found in
the finale, which starts with just first and second violins playing *piano*. Mozart again demonstrated his knowledge of the musical trends that would find favour with Parisian audiences, and
in an almost scornful account of its first performance, wrote '[T]he audience, as I expected,
said "hush" at the soft beginning, and when they heard the *forte*, began at once to clap their
hands.'[3] In addition to the recurring *coup d'archet*, the structure of the symphony itself follows
the trend in Paris at the time for three-movement symphonies (it was not yet the French convention to include a Minuet and Trio). In response to the audience's reception of it, Mozart did
later replace the original $\frac{6}{8}$ Andantino second movement (which was accused of having 'too
many modulations' and being 'too long' by the director of the *Concert Spirituel*, Jean Le Gros)
with a $\frac{3}{4}$ Andante.[4]

Beethoven and the idea of the freelance symphonist

Like Haydn, Beethoven was employed by a wealthy patron – the Elector of Bonn, Maximilian
Franz – primarily as court organist. Unlike Haydn, however, the younger composer did not
remain in this position for long. By the age of 17 he was sent to Vienna to study with Mozart,
but it is unclear whether the two composers actually met. In 1790, when Haydn was passing

2　　Neal Zaslaw, 'Mozart's Paris Symphonies', *The Musical Times*, 119/1627 (1978), 753–757.
3　　Zaslaw, 'Mozart's Paris Symphonies', 753.
4　　Zaslaw, 'Mozart's Paris Symphonies', 754.

through Bonn, Beethoven showed him some of his compositions. Two years later, Beethoven made the decisive move to Vienna in order to study composition with Haydn, counterpoint with Albrechtsberger, and Italian poetry-setting with Salieri. His patron, Count Waldstein, encouraged him to do so, writing 'You will receive the spirit of Mozart from the hands of Haydn' (it had to be Haydn's hands because Mozart had died the previous year).[5] By this stage, Beethoven was already securing a freelance income through various means, including sponsorship from patrons such as Prince Karl von Lichnowsky as well as the sale of works to publishers. Beethoven studied with Haydn for almost two years and remained in Vienna for much of the rest of his life, largely thanks to an unprecedented financial arrangement provided jointly by Prince Franz Joseph von Lobkowitz, Prince Kinsky, and Archduke Rudolph, which allowed the composer a lifetime allowance simply to stay in Vienna. Beethoven's music proved to be extremely popular with members of the nobility, leading to various means of patronage outside of the long-term employment that Mozart had sought.

Standard practice in the eighteenth century was for composers to dedicate their compositions to one another. Such was the case with Haydn's 'Mozart' quartets and Mozart's 'Haydn' quartets. Beethoven, however, also shrewdly dedicated works to the patrons who were supporting him, making it more likely that these patrons would offer financial support in the future. This can be seen across his catalogue of compositions, but we will of course focus on his symphonic output. One of the patrons who appears on the title page of many of Beethoven's instrumental works is Prince Lobkowitz. As well as providing financial security to Beethoven so that he could remain in Vienna, Lobkowitz was a keen patron of music and a supporter of Haydn and Beethoven. He created a grand concert hall at his palace and hired his own orchestra. As thanks for allowing the première performance to be held in this concert hall, Beethoven dedicated his Third Symphony in E♭ major, known as the 'Eroica', to the prince (having originally made the dedication to Napoleon Bonaparte – a decision he later rescinded). This arrangement clearly paid off, as Beethoven went on to dedicate his Fifth and Sixth Symphonies to Lobkowitz, which were premièred in the same concert in December 1808. A second name was added to the dedications for the latter two symphonies – Count Razumovsky (Lobkowitz's brother-in-law) – another patron of Beethoven's whose name is also given to his three string quartets, Op. 59. Count Moritz von Fries was another who, similar to Lobkowitz, was able to offer exposure in the form of various private concerts given at his family residence, the Palais Fries. Through these prestigious events, Moritz von Fries supported many musicians and composers including Haydn, Beethoven, and Schubert. As well as dedicating two sonatas for piano and violin (Op. 23 and Op. 24) and a string quintet (Op. 29) to him, Beethoven also cited the Count on the dedication for his Seventh Symphony.

Other patrons offered support in different ways. Baron Gottfried van Swieten was a long-standing patron to several prominent composers including Haydn and Mozart. As opposed to offering a salary or allowance, as was the case with Lobkowitz, Swieten offered occasional payments to the young composer, not unlike a modern-day tip. His support for these composers often went beyond financial means, even extending to offering artistic suggestions to Haydn about the setting of the text of his oratorio, *The Creation*. Swieten was an early patron

5   Charles Rosen, *The Classical Style*, 1971 [rev. 2005], 19.

of Beethoven's at the start of his Vienna years, and Beethoven dedicated his First Symphony to him. Prince Karl Lichnowsky was a significant supporter of Beethoven, even offering him a set of rooms in his own apartment in Vienna. Beethoven referred to him as 'one of my most loyal friends and promoters of my art', and it is easy to see why – Lichnowsky offered financial support in the form of a 600-florin annual allowance.[6] It is therefore perhaps unsurprising that Beethoven dedicated his Second Symphony to the prince.

The symphonies discussed so far were made possible by the financial support of various patrons, and this support and friendship allowed Beethoven some artistic independence. In the case of his Fourth and Ninth Symphonies, he received specific commissions. However, thanks to his reputation and the role he had constructed as a freelance composer, Beethoven was still able to maintain the freedom to compose as he wished. After a visit to Grätz with Prince Lichnowsky, the composer encountered Count Franz von Oppersdorff at his estate in nearby Silesia. Oppersdorff had his own accomplished court orchestra and was a keen patron of music. After a successful performance of Beethoven's Second Symphony by the court orchestra, Oppersdorff commissioned a new work. As part of the arrangement, the Count was able to hold the score to Beethoven's Fourth Symphony exclusively for six months, before Beethoven went on to publish it with a dedication to his newest patron. Oppersdorff paid a further sum of money to the composer for another symphony, the Fifth, but the work was dedicated to Razumovsky and Lobkowitz.

In spite of the fact that he was unable to gain employment and therefore security with a court appointment, Beethoven earned his living as a true freelance musician. A varied career of teaching, performing, and publishing his own compositions was supplemented by the support of several wealthy patrons, allowing him the financial backing to pursue commissions and compose music free from restrictions.

The invention of the concert hall

At a time when tensions between the social classes were running high (this was, after all, around the time of the French Revolution), a renewed interest in the pursuit of learning became more widespread, creating a new audience for art, literature, and music. Although private concerts remained the preserve of the extremely wealthy, underpinned by aristocratic support, public subscription concert series became increasingly popular among the growing middle class, where audience members paid for a season of concerts, and London became the leader in this trend. Wealthy members of the middle class would often attend several concerts per week, and in the late eighteenth century London was a bustling city and leading cultural hub. Large concert halls sprung up, such as the Hanover Square Rooms (built in 1775), and with this a new endeavour was born. Promoters such as Joseph Salomon commissioned works from well-known composers to satisfy the typical concert-goer, keen to immerse themselves in culture and the arts. Musical life became dominated by these public concerts, leading to the establishment of societies such as the London Philharmonic Society, dedicated to commissioning music to suit the tastes of the London audiences. Haydn's Symphony No. 104, Beethoven's Ninth,

---

6   Artur Pereira, *Beethoven's Dedications* (Abingdon and New York: Taylor & Francis, 2020), 179.

and Mendelssohn's Fourth, the 'Italian', were all commissioned by such concert societies in London. The success of these series led to the symphony becoming a key genre in London's musical culture.

Following the trend that started in London, many European cities introduced subscription concerts. Until then, concert organisers would have had to hire private salons on a regular basis, which proved costly. A subscription format was more financially viable, and extremely popular with members of the public wishing to indulge their appreciation of music and culture. This new concert culture was so popular that audiences were made up not only of the rising middle class, but also of members of the aristocracy and even (in London) by members of the royal family. Concerts were advertised, promoted, and reviewed in newspapers, so it was important that composers wrote music to suit the tastes of the paying audience. The growing public concert culture also led to the practice of repeat performances of works. This had a number of important consequences. First, it meant that new works were heard side-by-side with older ones, resulting in a greater historical awareness among listeners as well as composers. Secondly, the prospect of more than one performance of a composition gave composers a reason to be more daring and experimental: there was now no need for an audience to understand a symphony on a single hearing (think of Mozart and his 'Paris' Symphony) – they could hear the work multiple times and get something different from it on subsequent hearings. Lastly, it was an important contributor to the concept of a canon of symphonies that would remain permanently in the repertoire, and once this canon became established in the concert hall around the middle of the nineteenth century, repeat performances would help to sustain it until the present day.

Like his Fourth and Fifth Symphonies, Beethoven's final symphonic offering, the Ninth Symphony, was also a commission. In this case, however, it was commissioned not by an individual patron but by the Philharmonic Society of London (now the Royal Philharmonic Society) in 1817. It was premièred in 1824 in Vienna, and then received its British première almost a year later at the Argyll Rooms in London, a large venue capable of seating an audience of 650. In keeping with the London audiences' taste for Italian opera, the text of Schiller's *Ode to Joy* in the last movement was translated into Italian for this performance. The ticket sales for this capacity meant more money could be spent on the orchestra, facilitating a trend for more instruments and larger forces. For example, Beethoven's Ninth includes strings, double woodwind (plus piccolo and contrabassoon), nine brass players, and four percussionists, as well as four soloists and a choir. The entire work is around 70 minutes in performance, reflecting the larger proportions in London concert culture. By the 1830s the London Philharmonic Society could host an audience of 800 in their new larger concert hall at Hanover Square. The society commissioned Mendelssohn's 'Italian' Symphony in 1831, and it was premièred in London in 1833 in a concert that also contained Haydn's Symphony No. 104.

The idea of the symphony as a public-spirited genre grew in strength through the nineteenth century. Many composers looked to Beethoven not only for technical strategies on how to approach such a project, but also for an overarching philosophy that would guide the tradition. The idea of massed orchestral forces performing in front of a massed audience was new in Beethoven's time and represented a clean break from the system of aristocratic patronage that prevailed in the eighteenth century. This practice was aligned with the ethos of the French

Revolution: music should be for everyone, not just for the super-rich, and the growth of phil-harmonic societies and state institutions such as conservatories began the process of moving away from the eighteenth-century aristocratic model which had been overthrown in France.

The last decades of the nineteenth century saw yet further enlargements to concert venues for paying public audiences that were able to house the vastly expanded orchestras now being called upon by late-romantic and early-modernist symphonists. Gustav Mahler's symphonic output in the last decade of the century calls for a massive orchestra. His Second Symphony (first performed in 1895) requires quadruple wind, 25 brass players, two sets of timpani (played by three players) as part of a very large percussion section, chorus, vocal soloists, organ, and 'the largest possible contingent of all strings'.[7] We should remember, how-ever, that professional concert series remained a stubbornly elite pastime, even 100 years after the old system of aristocratic patronage had begun to break down. Although public concerts were theoretically available to anyone able to pay for a ticket and were no longer the preserve of the aristocracy, ticket prices remained out of reach for the vast majority of the ordinary city-dwelling population of Vienna, and would even have been considered expensive for the middle classes.[8] The types of repertoire on offer in these concerts also took on political over-tones, with the older and more established liberal order aligning itself with Brahms, while the new political forces, coming mainly from the right, tethered themselves to performances of Bruckner's symphonies, with their strong associations with Wagner and by extension his own right-wing politics.

By the end of the nineteenth century, many of the concert halls that would sustain large-scale orchestral performances and provide homes for professional orchestras for the next 150 years had already been built. In the city of London, we have one of the greatest success stories of any concert hall in the world, as well as one of the institution's greatest tragedies. Beginning with the latter, the Queen's Hall was under construction in the early 1890s and opened its doors for the first time in 1893. It stood in Langham Place in London's West End, close to where the BBC studios are currently housed, and it was widely reported to have had a beautifully resonant acoustic. At a capacity of about 2,500, the hall was one of the largest in the world at the time and would become the home of the BBC Symphony Orchestra and the London Philharmonic Orchestra, as well as the principal venue for premières of new works. It was also the home of a newly launched summer music festival, inaugurated in 1895 and performed by the Queen's Hall Orchestra conducted by Henry Wood. This is the concert series that we now know as The Proms. Then, as now, it provided the opportunity for audiences to attend semi-formal concerts during the summer months with low ticket prices, and the festival continues to attract the best orchestras in the world today. The Queen's Hall remained the foremost concert venue in the UK well into the twentieth century. After being damaged during air raids in 1940 and 1941, a bomb landed directly on the building on May 10th that year, completely destroying the auditor-ium, beyond any hope of repair. While there were initial plans to rebuild the hall, these ran into administrative and financial difficulties, and eventually the project was abandoned.

7   Gustav Mahler, *Zweite Symphonie* (Leipzig: Universal, 1897), 2. The German original reads: 'Alle in möglichst starker besetzung'.
8   Margaret Notley, '"Volksconcerte" in Vienna and Late Nineteenth-Century Ideology of the Symphony', *Journal of the American Musicological Society*, 50/2, 3 (1997), 421–453.

The tragedy of the Queen's Hall ended its time as the home of The Proms, but the festival's current home, the Royal Albert Hall, is one of the greatest success stories of any concert venue of the nineteenth century. The hall was opened by Queen Victoria in 1871. An unusual design by modern standards, it featured an oval-shaped central arena (complete with a fountain, which provided a focal point while also acting as a temperature regulator during the summer) surrounded by tiers of seating that can now accommodate over 5,000 audience members. The very high domed roof and the enormous proportions of the hall produce an unusual acoustic, but the hall remains one of the world's leading venues, as well as one of its most accessible: as of 2021, a Proms ticket for the arena costs only £7.00.

In this chapter we have assessed how and why the status of the symphony changed between the mid-eighteenth and late-nineteenth centuries. The key questions that have been raised relate to ideas of compositional freedom, the relationship between economic factors and musical content, and the importance of institutions such as philharmonic societies and concert venues in shaping the genre. These questions remain open: who had the greater musical freedom, the eighteenth-century *Kapellmeister*, or the nineteenth-century freelance composer? To what extent did the new market for public concerts impact on the musical content of symphonies? How important were Vienna, Paris, and London for the development of the genre? These questions are about musical contexts; however, as we shall see, they are also important for understanding the creative decisions that composers were making. In the next four chapters we will focus on these compositional decisions in a much more specific way as we consider issues of musical language, form, and structure.

POINTS FOR FURTHER DISCUSSION

- To what extent is the symphony an Italian invention?
- What role did the Mannheim School play in the invention and development of the symphony?
- How accurate is it to describe Joseph Haydn as the 'father of the symphony'?
- What role did the public concert play in the development of the symphony?
- Who had the greater musical freedom – Joseph Haydn or Ludwig van Beethoven? How is this represented in their symphonic output?

Part II: Materials

4
Melody, harmony, and syntax

Symphonies have a dual existence. They are, of course, objects of history that were created in the past. They have their own compositional, cultural, and historical contexts, as well as reception histories that were often played out as messy political or aesthetic debates and controversies. Symphonies also exist in the present, however. They form a part of modern concert repertoires and educational curricula, and therefore require a modern response. They exist as texts that persist through time and we need to construct languages for referring to them and approaches which help to increase our understanding of them. This is the job of music theory and analysis, to which we will now turn our attention.

Classical harmony

Concert music in the eighteenth and nineteenth centuries was composed using a system of pitch relations that we refer to as **tonality**. Tonal music organises the 12 notes of the chromatic scale into a system of relationships that all ultimately relate back to a central point of reference, or **tonic**. Although any note of the chromatic scale can be used as the central tonic, some are used much more often than others. The tonic provides the coordinates for organising each of the other notes into a series of relations with one another – these might be intervals, chords, or scales – which we call a **key**. Some notes in a particular key are in a close relationship with the tonic, whereas others are considered to be more distant. No pitch within the 12-note Western system is ever 'unrelated' – everything, no matter how distant it might seem, is in some way related to everything else. This system forms the foundation for pitch organisation in the repertoire that we are interested in here.

The two modes that were used in the period 1750–1900 were **major** and **minor**, and the mode the composer chooses affects the relationship between notes within a key. These are not to be confused with the church modes associated with early music (mixolydian, dorian, phrygian, etc.). The major and minor modes carry with them different sets of conventions and associations. The major mode is typically used to convey positive, peaceful, playful, energetic, heroic, or triumphant moods, for example, whereas the minor mode is more often used for negative, melancholic, troubled, stormy, or tragic music.

FIG. 4.1 NOTES OF THE MAJOR AND MINOR SCALES AND THEIR RELATIONSHIP TO THE TONIC

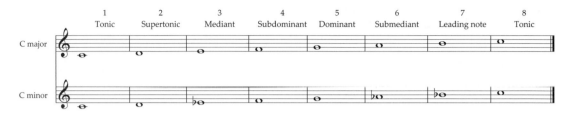

Each note of any major or minor scale can be turned into a chord by adding a third and a fifth above it. As well as using Roman numerals to describe these chords, each triad can be expressed in a number of different inversions, which we use figured bass to notate (second inversions are discords and are therefore not shown in **FIG. 4.2**).

FIG. 4.2 TRIADIC HARMONY AS EXPRESSED IN MAJOR AND MINOR KEYS, ROMAN NUMERALS, AND FIRST INVERSIONS

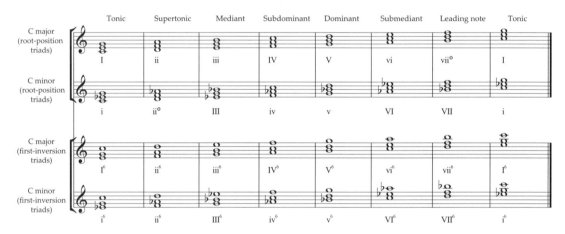

Just as the notes of the scale, whether minor or major, are each related to a tonic, and each of these notes produces a chord that can be related to the central tonic triad (using Roman numerals) so each of these harmonies can be treated as a temporary tonic. This procedure, commonly referred to as **modulation**, occurs when the music seems to move from one key to another. A more accurate term for this idea is **tonicisation**, in which the new key is treated as a tonic in its own right – a temporary tonic with its own system of harmonic relations – before eventually returning to the overarching home tonic where the music began.

Cadence as musical punctuation

Music is not a language – you can't order a pizza using a piece of instrumental music, for example – but sometimes it appears to act like one. An example of this is music's use of common structures that express finality. These structures behave as punctuation does in written language – full stops, commas, and question marks. As in language, punctuation is important in music because it gives musical ideas a sense of structure and order. Any idea expressed in language without the use of punctuation would quickly become slippery in its meaning, verging on nonsense, and the same is true, at least in the eighteenth century, for music. For our purposes, there are two varieties of musical punctuation that were used to articulate musical ideas in the decades around 1800. These were the 'perfect cadence' and the 'imperfect cadence'.

The **perfect cadence** is a way of expressing finality. It consists of a motion from root-position dominant harmony (V) to a root-position tonic (I), and this would nearly always coincide with a metrically strong point in the bar and in the broader phrase. The effect is further strengthened if the cadence is followed by a break, rest, or pause, or by moving on to new material. The sense of finality provided by the perfect cadence is at its strongest when motion in the melody is directed by step towards the tonic as it coincides with the motion from V to I in the bass. The dominant in this case would either support the leading note or the supertonic. When all three conditions are met (chord V followed by chord I; both chords in root position; and stepwise motion towards the tonic in the melody) then the structure produces the strongest possible indicator of finality in the tonal system. When the first two conditions are met, but the melody does not reach the tonic by step, this indicates a weaker degree of finality.

EX. 4.1 HAYDN, SYMPHONY NO. 94 IN G, 'SURPRISE', IV, BARS 1–8

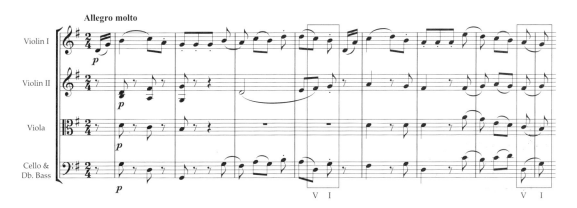

This example from Haydn shows how he creates different degrees of finality in his theme by using first a perfect cadence in bar 4 at the mid-point, temporarily coming to rest in the melody on scale degree three, B. He saves the more emphatic cadence for the end, with root position V followed by I supporting the tonic in the melody in bar 8.

There are other ways in which composers might express finality by using dynamics, articulation, orchestration, tempo, and repetition, but these are often used for emphasis or confirmation. Without the fundamental harmonic and melodic ingredients of musical punctuation there can be no real sense of finality within the tonal system.

The other type of cadence commonly used in this repertoire is the 'half-cadence' or **imperfect cadence**. This is identified by its key ingredient, an arrival on root position dominant harmony (chord V). As with the perfect cadence, the imperfect cadence typically lands on a metrically strong part of the bar and is similarly strengthened when followed by a rest or a break in the texture. Its effect is not quite as easily compared with the punctuation we find in language as is the perfect cadence. The imperfect cadence expresses the end of a phrase of music, but it also strongly implies that there is more to follow. Analogies have been made between the imperfect cadence and the comma, the full colon, and the question mark, and each of these analogies might be valid.

EX. 4.2 AN IMPERFECT CADENCE IN MOZART'S 'LINZ' SYMPHONY, NO. 36 IN C, K. 425, II, BARS 1–4

One of the most common places you will find an imperfect cadence is halfway through a theme. We can see in **EX. 4.2** that Mozart's theme arrives on chord V in bar 4. Listening to a performance of this example, you'll notice that it generates a slight sense of finality but also implies there is more to be done. This is typical of the imperfect cadence: it partly rounds off one idea while also suggesting further material that might serve to work out the idea more fully and eventually to complete it with a perfect cadence. The imperfect cadence is sometimes used rather more emphatically at important structural points within a piece of music, most commonly to announce the arrival of a new theme, or the return of a theme that has been absent for a long time.

The structure of eighteenth-century melody

Thematic material in the classical period was organised in quite a different way to that of the late baroque. To explain this, let's start with a counterexample. In late-baroque music it was conventional to begin with a musical idea (let's call it a basic idea) and then to use a technique called ***Fortspinnung***. This German term literally means to 'spin forth' an idea by repeating it over and over in sequence, often very inventively, resulting eventually in some sort of cadence, often in a new key. This process can be quite exciting, largely because there is no convention to indicate for how long the process should continue. Each time it occurs it could be unique in terms of phrase length. The process could result in a three-bar phrase, or it could be seven bars, or eight, or 11, or 17. It depends on the nature of the musical idea that the composer has started with.

J. S. Bach's Violin Concerto in A minor (**EX. 4.3**) is a good example of this procedure, in which the four-bar basic idea is spun out over 20 bars of continuous *Fortspinnung* before the music reaches a cadence. This can be compared and contrasted with the regularity and conventionality of melodic phrasing that was characteristic in the later part of the eighteenth century, during which time the music seemed to group into neat two-bar ideas, four-bar phrases, and eight- or 12-bar themes. Let's look at two of the most common ways that classical composers organised their thematic material: the **sentence** and the **period**.

The **sentence** is a unit of musical organisation that is more substantial than a 'motive', a 'figure' or an 'idea', and is one of the most common constituents of classical themes. It consists of three basic components:

1. The **presentation** offers the characteristic thematic material that might be repeated once, twice, or more times, and which consists of one or more shorter motives.
2. The **continuation**, as the name suggests, continues the material often by breaking it up into its smaller components (sometimes called 'fragmentation') while increasing the rate of harmonic change and rhetorical intensity (e.g., louder dynamics, shorter note values, and busier texture).
3. The process of fragmentation leads to a **cadence** – either perfect or imperfect – in which the characteristic material from the opening presentation is usually absent.

The primary theme of **Beethoven's First Symphony in C, Op. 21**, provides a clear example of this process (see **EX. 4.4**).

In this case, the dotted figure (motive x) is the most characteristic and identifiable thematic material which Beethoven uses in this movement, while the upward arpeggio (motive y) and the chromatic motion in the woodwind (motive z) provide some complementary linking material. Motives x, y, and z form the first **presentation** in bars 13–18, outlining the tonic, C major. Beethoven then offers this same presentation of the motivic material again in bars 19–24, this time up a step, outlining D minor (chord ii). Bars 25–30 provide the **continuation** of this material by intensifying it (in this case by increasing the dynamics, articulation, and scoring), by fragmenting it (motives y and z seem to have disappeared and we are left with lots of presentations of motive x in quick succession), and by standing on an expectant dominant harmony which suggests forward motion. By bar 31 motive x seems also to have disappeared and Beethoven provides a **perfect cadence** in C major via a series of loud tutti chords which, on their own, could not be used to identify the symphony. This is typical of cadences, which tend to be very generic. The same could be said about punctuation in language – though we might claim to connect words together in unique ways, no one could say the full stop they used was unlike anyone else's!

The other unit of musical organisation common in the late eighteenth century is the **period**, which differs from the sentence in some important ways, and which is frequently composed of two sentences, one answering the other. Periods are often regular, lasting eight bars resulting from two four-bar phrases. The first of these phrases presents the motivic material and results in an imperfect cadence. This sets up a return to the opening material once again, but this second phrase usually achieves a stronger cadence (most frequently a perfect cadence). The conventional method of achieving this perfect cadence is to intensify the material so as to reach the dominant harmony slightly earlier, leaving enough space in the fixed four-bar metrical framework to fit in both V and I instead of only reaching V. In a case such as this, the first phrase which achieves an imperfect cadence is called an **antecedent** and the second phrase which closes with a perfect cadence is called a **consequent**.

EX. 4.3 *FORTSPINNUNG* IN THE OPENING RITORNELLO OF J. S. BACH'S VIOLIN CONCERTO
IN A MINOR, BWV 1041, BARS 1–24

EX. 4.4 AN EXAMPLE OF A MUSICAL SENTENCE FROM BEETHOVEN, SYMPHONY NO. 1 IN C, OP. 21, I, BARS 13–33

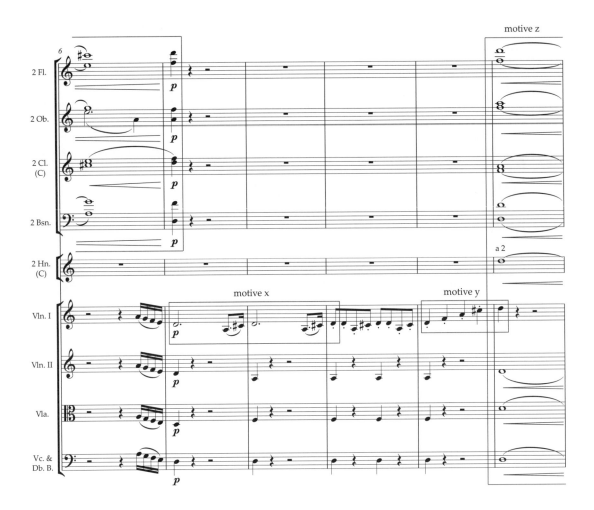

cadence

FIG. 4.3 A SCHEMATIC DIAGRAM OF A MUSICAL PERIOD

Antecedent			Consequent		
Presentation of basic idea	Continuation, intensification	Imperfect cadence	Presentation of basic idea	Continuation, intensification	Perfect cadence
I		V	I		V I

EX. 4.5 A PERIOD FROM MENDELSSOHN, SYMPHONY NO. 4 IN A, OP. 90, 'ITALIAN', II, BARS 2–11

These methods of organising thematic materials were not particular to the classical era. They continued to be used long into the nineteenth century, and **EX. 4.5** shows a period by **Mendelssohn** from his **Fourth Symphony, the 'Italian'**. This is a very clear case of a typical period in which the first four bars act as an antecedent, setting up an arrival on V (an imperfect cadence), and then the consequent phrase closes the theme in the tonic with a perfect cadence in D minor.

One of Mendelssohn's projects as a composer was to continue the symphonic tradition as he had inherited it from Haydn, Mozart, and Beethoven. Rather than trying to preserve an old-fashioned style that had been popular 50 years before his time, however, he aimed to continue the process of invention and innovation. There are many ways in which Mendelssohn developed the classical style. For now, let's consider a representative example from the same symphony, this time from the first movement (**EX. 4.6**).

◆ ◆ ◆

CASE STUDY: SYMPHONY NO. 4 IN A, 'ITALIAN' (1833–4) BY FELIX MENDELSSOHN

This theme in E major initially sets up an antecedent phrase resulting in an arrival on V. This already goes beyond classical norms because at 14 bars in length the phrase is metrically irregular. Still, it would be possible here to construct a consequent that closes with a perfect cadence in E major (the temporary tonic at this point in the piece). Mendelssohn, however, had other ideas. Instead of producing a cadence and closing the theme, the music seems to abandon this idea altogether and return to the material from the beginning of the movement. Even this is not enough to produce closure, and a full 60 bars of further tonal argument is required before a perfect cadence can be produced. This is an example of **cadential deferral**, in which the point of musical punctuation is delayed beyond the range of the theme that was supposed to produce it. The result of this technique is a much more continuous syntax in which musical arguments are not divided up neatly into regular phrases but stretch out and expand into much longer paragraphs.

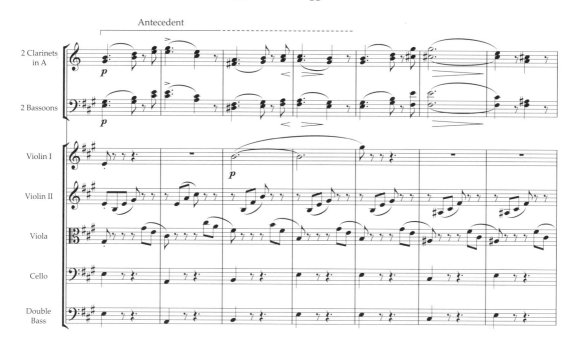

Wagner's influence: 'unending melody'

Wagner only completed one symphony, and it is performed quite infrequently – he is much better known for his music dramas. However, he is considered by music historians and theorists to be a pivotal figure who was largely responsible for the widespread change of style that occurred in the middle of the nineteenth century. The impact this had on composition can be detected in the work of important late-nineteenth-century symphonists such as Bruckner, Tchaikovsky, and Mahler. Related to the massively expanded harmonic and tonal palette that Wagner used in his music is the overhaul of classical conventions of syntax. This especially relates to classical notions of balance (such as the 4+4=8 metrical ordering of periodic structures) and closure (classical themes tend to have a well-defined beginning, middle, and end, with a cadence used for punctuation). Unlike Mendelssohn who saw himself as the inheritor of the Mozartian tradition of instrumental composition, Wagner claimed that the symphony had run its course, which is why Beethoven had made the leap to using a text by Schiller (the famous *Ode to Joy*) sung by a choir and a quartet of soloists in his Ninth Symphony. The logical next step for Wagner, then, was to compose operas as a way of continuing the Beethovenian tradition, which had culminated in the Ninth Symphony. In other words, embracing text and the voice was for Wagner now a necessary vehicle for musical expression.

One of the techniques Wagner used in his music dramas was the so-called **unending melody** in which, as the name suggests, the melodic line seems to continue at length without coming to rest with a cadence. The classic example of this can be found in (probably) Wagner's darkest work, *Tristan und Isolde*, whose substantial prelude (see **EX. 4.7**) does not contain a single perfect cadence – not even at the very end. It simply continues, violating the central classical principle of tonal closure.

EX. 4.7 THE OPENING OF THE PRELUDE TO WAGNER'S *TRISTAN UND ISOLDE*, BARS 1–3

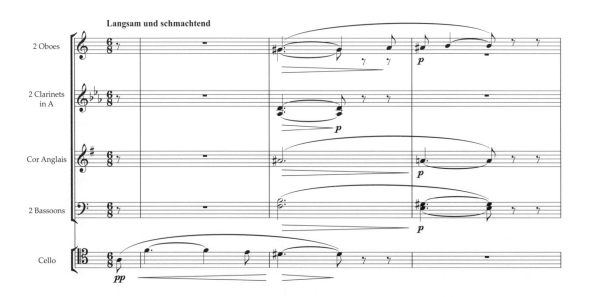

Given this music performs a very specific function as the opening to an opera, it may seem an impossible task to use this compositional method in the context of a symphony, which would ordinarily not have a text, an overt plot, or even any characters to create direction and meaning. Nevertheless, Anton Bruckner (1824–1896), who was a deep admirer of Wagner's music, absorbed this type of new musical syntax into his style and used it in increasingly extensive ways. It is possible in Bruckner's output to find whole symphonic movements which contain no perfect cadences at all, and this extreme control of tonal closure is stretched strategically across whole symphonies, sometimes lasting well over an hour in performance. One of the results of this sparing use of cadences is that when one does arrive it is treated as a very big deal!

Tchaikovsky was a master of the emotionally loaded 'if only!' in his symphonies, and these moments often hinge on the failure of the music to produce a cadence and to secure its tonality. A clear example of this can be heard in his **Sixth Symphony in B minor, the 'Pathétique'** (1893) (**EX. 4.8**). This theme has the opportunity to generate closure with a strong perfect cadence in D major, but after repeated opportunities the melody resolutely refuses to descend to D, instead resting on the fifth scale degree (A) while the bass never touches on V. The overtly tragic theme in this work, and the composer's mysterious death shortly after the première, provide a context which supports such a reading – namely that the part of the movement that is set in the major mode, with all of the positive connotations it brings, is unable to secure its own tonality with a perfect cadence.

EX. 4.8 THE LYRICAL THEME IS UNABLE TO CLOSE IN TCHAIKOVSKY, SYMPHONY NO. 6 IN B MINOR, 'PATHÉTIQUE', I, BARS 153–160

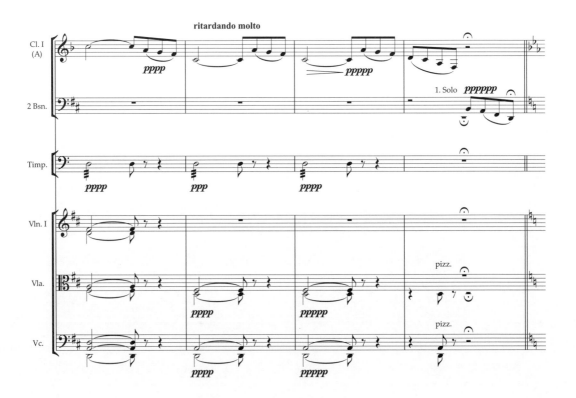

Brahms and 'developing variation'

Another way that melodic organisation became more expansive and complex during the nineteenth century was through a technique called **'developing variation'**. Although it can be traced back at least as far as Beethoven, the clearest examples are evident in Brahms's music. Unlike Wagner's constantly changing melodies that continuously evade closure, Brahms's technique was to use a very small amount of melodic material – sometimes just a few notes – and progressively to change its use by making very small variations to it. Each of these variations might be barely perceptible on their own. The change might just be by one note at a time. However, the effect over a longer span is a little like watching the minute hand of a clock: you can't see it move, but after some time has elapsed you notice it is in a different place. Brahms's music often gives the effect of developing its material so subtly that it is impossible to tell where one melody ends and another begins. Part of the reason behind this comes from the influence Brahms drew from much older music, especially the type of renaissance polyphonic music he engaged as a scholar, as well as J. S. Bach's contrapuntal writing. Brahms viewed himself as operating within a direct line of influence from Bach through Haydn, Beethoven, Mendelssohn, and Schumann, and it is therefore no wonder that the principle of developing variation, which is comparable with the *Fortspinnung* technique discussed at the beginning of this chapter, is so richly expressed in Brahms's music.

Brahms's Fourth Symphony in E minor exhibits this type of melodic organisation. In the case of the first movement (**EX. 4.9**) we can see that the theme is constructed as a series of falling thirds (and occasionally the music ascends a sixth in order to maintain the same register). Part of the technique is to try to use up as much potential in the material as possible before moving on, and as you can see, Brahms visits every single note in the E minor scale once before repeating a single note. When the music gets back to the tonic again, Brahms repeats the process, this time ascending through the major thirds, visiting each note once. This technique of using small, abstract melodic units to build up a longer melody has been described as a kind of musical prose owing to the sense of continuity it produces and the scarcity of punctuation. Eventually, of course, the music comes to a point of arrival which is articulated with a cadence (in this case an imperfect cadence), but it does not feature the sort of repetition and rhyming cadences we find in classical structures such as the period, for example. Developing variation, therefore, is a technique that allows a much more expansive melodic statement to unfold while at the same time being very efficient with the thematic material, often recycling the initial idea many times with only tiny changes to it along the way in order to produce a long paragraph of continuous melody.

5
Form, structure, and cycle

In the last chapter we examined how the tonal system operates together with melody, harmony, and bass in order to produce a set of conventions that were common among composers working in Vienna in the late eighteenth century. We have seen how techniques such as repetition and closure serve to articulate musical ideas, and we have also observed how these classical principles were expanded, developed, stretched, and even rejected during the nineteenth century. Now that we have a basic understanding of tonal and thematic musical language, or syntax, we can apply these ideas at the larger scale by looking at musical forms. We will consider the overarching structure of the symphony and look briefly at some of the common forms found in the second, third, and fourth movements.

Symphonic music operates on lots of different levels. The arrangement of the movements within a complete work is called a **cycle**. Each of those individual movements has a **form** (e.g., rondo or sonata form) and each form is composed of a number of **sections**, for example, an exposition section, which is composed of yet smaller units of music. By around 1770, the symphony had begun to gel into a set format consisting of four movements. The success of this four-movement cycle relies on a delicate balance of contrast and unity. The contrast within the work is generated by a variety of tempos, keys, metres, textures, colours, and forms between the different movements. Composers didn't just write one thing after another, though. It was necessary to have a thread running throughout to unify the different movements. The main way of unifying a long work like a symphony was to begin and end in the same key, with the option of visiting contrasting keys along the way. While there are many examples of symphonies by Haydn, Mozart, and Beethoven that contain different numbers of movements, the four-movement plan should be considered a default option in the last decades of the eighteenth century, and any deviation from this pattern should be read against it. For example, Mozart's 'Paris' Symphony contains only three movements, so we need to ask what set of musical or cultural contexts led to his decision to omit the Minuet. Schumann's Third Symphony, the 'Rhenish', is composed of five movements, so we have to ask what conditions led him to insert a further slow movement before the finale. Before we can begin to answer these questions, we need to establish what the standard pattern of the classical period was, and how it operates. We say 'standard' not because it is the 'best' way of doing things – it is simply a statistical fact that the canonical repertoire of symphonies from the Viennese tradition around 1800 was organised in this way.

The four-movement symphony

This was the normal way of organising a symphony around 1800. The work was organised into four parts or 'movements', like the chapters of a book, which generally followed an established plan:

1. A **fast-tempo first movement** establishes the key, mode (major or minor), and mood of the work as a whole. This movement is almost always in sonata form (see Chapter 6), which was considered obligatory. It contains the 'serious' material of the work; most symphonies before 1800 are considered to be 'front-weighted' and the first movement is usually the longest and the most complex.
2. A **slow second movement** is in a contrasting key; subdominant, dominant, and relative major or minor are common choices, though more adventurous options do exist. This movement gives the opportunity for a lyrical or reflective contrast of mood compared with the more dramatic first movement. There is sometimes a change of mode, especially if the first movement was in a minor key (therefore offering a more optimistic alternative mood at this point). The choice of form is also up to the individual composer, and no one form is considered obligatory.
3. A **Minuet and Trio** provides a return to the tonic key, a faster tempo, and is in a very strictly obligatory form (discussed below).
4. A **fast finale** confirms the tonic key and is usually more light-hearted than the previous movements. It might be humorous or witty, and it is common to find some impressive or triumphant flourishes, particularly towards the end.

While there are deviations, the majority of classical symphonies from Haydn onwards follow a version of this plan. One of the main benefits of the four-movement cycle is that it offers the opportunity to create a contrast between the first two movements by moving away from the tonic key and by changing tempo before returning to the tonic and a fast tempo by the end of the work. This helps to generate unity – a sense that the four movements belong together.

Binary and ternary forms

These forms had been in development during the eighteenth century and earlier. Binary form was common in a lot of instrumental music from the time of J. S. Bach, Handel, and Scarlatti, while ternary form had been a standard strategy in both instrumental and vocal music, especially in opera where the 'da capo' aria was an important vehicle for expression and improvisation for the soloists. These forms found their way into the classical symphony and were regularly used as the basis for the inner movements (that is, the slow second movement and the Minuet and Trio).

Binary form, as the name suggests, is composed of two broad paragraphs of music. The first of these moves from the tonic of the movement to a related key (usually V if the piece is in the major mode, or III if in the minor mode). The second half of the form then charts a path from where it left off back to the tonic, and it will usually recycle the material outlined in the first half. It therefore produces quite a concentrated focus on a single mood while generating contrast through its key structure. The convention is to repeat each of the two parts of the binary form, and so it is usually quite easy to identify by looking at the score or by listening to the repeat structure (**FIG. 5.1**).

FIG. 5.1 SCHEMATIC DIAGRAM OF BINARY FORM

'Open' structure   'Closed' structure
Motion from I to V (or III)   Motion from V to I (or i)

Ternary form is quite different from binary form because it is fundamentally a way of generating thematic and tonal contrast, rather than maintaining a single mood for the duration of the movement. Ternary form consists of an opening section – let's call it the 'A' section – which is closed in its key. This is followed by a contrasting 'B' section in a different key and with new thematic material. This B section is sometimes closed in its own key, but is frequently left open, ending on an imperfect cadence and preparing the return of the A section, which will usually have some significant variation on the second hearing. Ternary form is therefore understood as being in three sections – ABA – in which the middle B section contrasts with the surrounding A sections in terms of key, mode, theme, mood, and even tempo in some cases (**FIG. 5.2**).

FIG. 5.2 SCHEMATIC DIAGRAM OF TERNARY FORM

A	B	A
'Closed' structure beginning and ending in I	'Open' structure exploring contrasting keys ending on V as a chord	'Closed' structure beginning and ending in I

Rounded binary, and Minuet and Trio

Rounded binary form is one of the most important building blocks in eighteenth-century music. It is the basis of the most common forms found in the symphonic repertoire, which include the Minuet and Trio, variation form, and rondo form (but not sonata form, which will be covered in Chapter 6). Rounded binary contains a mixture of ideas drawn from binary form and ternary form. Like binary form, it is divided into two parts that are usually easily identified because they are separated by double bars with dots. The first part presents the main idea of the piece. Let's call this 'a'.[1] After the double-bar a new idea is presented, which we'll call 'b'. Before the end, however, 'a' returns, usually in a modified or shortened format – in **FIG. 5.3** this

---

1   Upper-case letters are used for sections of a whole movement. Lower-case letters are used for the smaller building blocks of larger sections. The ternary form ABA would normally be a whole piece of music, whereas the rounded binary form aba' is usually a building block of a larger form.

is signified with a dash after the letter (a′). In one sense, then, this produces something that looks and sounds like ternary form (ABA); however, the repetition scheme and tonal plot give more of a sense of binary form. Unlike the simple ternary form in which the opening A section closes in the tonic key, several options exist within rounded binary form. The most straightforward is to remain in the same key. More dynamic options include leaving the idea open-ended with an imperfect cadence, or modulating to a new key (V if the piece is in the major mode, III if it's minor) and closing with a perfect cadence in that key. When 'a' returns towards the end of the form, it will be in the tonic and it nearly always closes with a perfect cadence in that key. The middle 'b' idea introduces some new, possibly contrasting, material, and it usually aims to produce an imperfect cadence in preparation for the return of 'a' and the tonic key (**FIG. 5.3**).

FIG. 5.3 SCHEMATIC DIAGRAM OF ROUNDED BINARY FORM

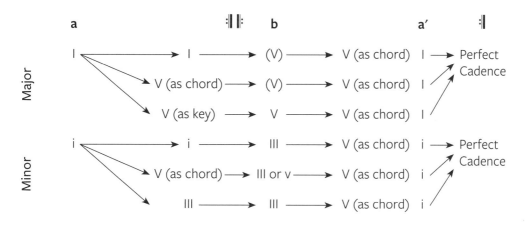

The main things that separate rounded binary form from simple ternary form, then, are:

1) The opening 'a' section has the option to move away from the tonic, whereas the A section of simple ternary form will always close in the tonic.
2) There is a strong convention in rounded binary form to repeat the two halves (a and ba′) with the use of repeat signs, whereas simple ternary form usually does not feature internal double bars.

The third movement is usually structured as a **Minuet and Trio**, that is to say, a stately dance in triple metre. The form of this type of dance movement is regarded as obligatory and consists of two rounded binary structures. The opening Minuet is organised in the way described above, followed by the Trio, which uses contrasting thematic material but is nevertheless structured in the same way. After the Trio, the Minuet is repeated, which produces a ternary structure on a much larger scale (see **FIG. 5.4**). This type of movement, then, can be understood as a series of binary and ternary structures operating at different levels of the form.

FIG. 5.4 SCHEMATIC DIAGRAM OF A MINUET AND TRIO

A Minuet	B Trio	A′ Minuet (da capo)
tonic	contrasting key tonic minor/subdominant/ dominant/relative	tonic
stately	contrasting mood	stately

As you can see from the model above, key relations between sections are crucial in the Minuet and Trio form. Whereas the standard route was to stick to tonic and dominant (and occasionally relative major/minor) key relations, **Haydn** found ways to play with this convention leading to a more adventurous harmonic structure. In the third movement of his **'London' Symphony, No. 104**, he included an additional linking passage at the end of the Trio. In this case the Trio is in B♭ major, the flattened submediant of the home key of D major. This presents a problem at the end of the Trio: jumping from B♭ major straight back to D major would be clunky. The linking passage therefore moves chromatically through a German augmented sixth chord before landing on a chord of A major (the dominant of D), ready for the repeat of the Minuet (see **TABLE 5.1**).

In the eighteenth-century Minuet and Trio, tempo markings could vary from a leisurely Moderato to a more lively Allegro. The more common Allegretto offered a gently lilting dance tempo that could either be felt as the traditional three beats in a bar or in a livelier one in a bar. Beethoven is largely credited with pioneering the transition from the stately Minuet to the more fiery **Scherzo** which came to replace it. The Scherzo is different from the Minuet in a number of ways. First, it is a much faster piece. Although moderate-tempo Scherzos do exist, the norm is a fast or very fast tempo, with options including Allegro, Allegro molto, Presto, Vivace, and Vivace molto. Secondly, the metre has a different flavour, with the music usually expressed in compound time, with options including $\frac{3}{8}$, $\frac{6}{8}$, and $\frac{12}{8}$. Frequently we find Scherzos set in the traditional $\frac{3}{4}$ metre, but at a faster tempo this is virtually impossible to distinguish from $\frac{3}{8}$ if the score is not visible to us. A good example of this is found in **Beethoven's Seventh Symphony**, in which Beethoven gives the tempo indication as 'Presto' and the metronome marking of ♩. = 132 (very fast indeed!). Compared with the classical Minuet, not only is it clearly much faster but it is also more playful, perhaps even insistent, in mood (see **EX. 5.1**).

TABLE 5.1 STRUCTURE OF HAYDN'S 'LONDON' SYMPHONY, NO. 104, III

Haydn, Symphony No. 104 in D major, third movement			
Minuet (in D major)	a (1–16)	b (17–34)	a' (35–52)
	The main idea of the movement is played twice and remains closed in the tonic, D major.	The contrasting middle of the Minuet moves through B minor before progressing to A major, setting up the return of the tonic.	The main idea is repeated with a stronger finish, enhanced by a rhetorical silence.
Trio (in B♭ major)	c (53–64)	d (65–78)	c' (79–94)
	The main idea of the trio contrasts with the Minuet. It is quieter and more reflective; it also contrasts in its tonality. The first section moves from B♭ to F major.	The middle of the trio briefly visits the temporary tonal centre of G before returning to B♭.	The repeat of the Trio's main idea also uses a rhetorical silence to aid its sense of finality, this time closing in B♭ major.
Retransitional link	(95–104)		
	A short link, using the main motivic idea of the Trio, is used to return to the key of D major through its dominant chord, A major.		
Minuet, *da capo*	a (1–16)	b (17–34)	a' (35–52)

While Haydn's Minuet and Trio signalled a move away from stately Minuets of the baroque dance suite and towards the more lively movement that would later develop into the Scherzo and Trio, Mendelssohn composed a more nostalgic, noble Minuet in his 'Italian' Symphony, recalling the classical model. He does, however, find ways to play with the form. In both the Minuet and the Trio, Mendelssohn expands the second half to generate increased harmonic development. He also includes a coda at the end of the movement, combining material from both the Minuet and the Trio.

EX. 5.1 BEETHOVEN, SYMPHONY NO. 7 IN A, OP. 92, III, BARS 1–10

Variation and episodic forms

The slow movement is the area of the symphony that offers the composer the largest degree of freedom in terms of form. Some slow movements have ternary designs (Beethoven's Third Symphony is a clear, though complex example) while others are organised in sonata form. **Sets of variations on a theme** were quite common for Haydn (and they can even be found in some fast finales: again, Beethoven's Third Symphony is a really clear and well-developed example). Sets of variations are most frequently based on a theme that is structured in rounded binary form (discussed above) in which each successive section adds increasingly complex variations through the use of shorter note values (diminutions), more decorative scoring, additional layers of counterpoint, and sometimes a shift of mode. This is the case in the second movement of **Haydn's Symphony No. 94 in G**, nicknamed the 'Surprise' because of the loud chord that occurs very suddenly at the end of the 'a' section of its opening rounded binary form. In this C major movement, Haydn introduces a variation in C minor, which brings with it a different set of tonal norms. All the variations in C major, as well as the theme itself, modulate to V by the first double bar. The C minor variation, however, modulates to III. This is normal for binary form in the minor mode, but it produces a modulation to E♭ major, which is quite distant from the home tonic of C major. It is therefore necessary for Haydn to extend the 'b' section of this variation in order to return to C major for the next rounded binary form.

Variation forms became less popular in slow movements during the nineteenth century, but they found a new home in the finale. Brahms used a passacaglia theme in the last movement of his Fourth Symphony that forms the basis of an extremely intensive set of variations drawing on the contrapuntal tradition of J. S. Bach and Buxtehude. The finale of Dvořák's (1841–1904) Eighth Symphony contains a more light-hearted set of variations (again based on a theme in rounded binary form) which bears comparison with the finale of Beethoven's Third.

It is also quite common to find more loosely organised variation forms with contrasting episodes that break up the harmonic and thematic repetition (one of the risks of a 'pure' variation movement). Tchaikovsky's Second Symphony in C minor, nicknamed the 'Little Russian', contains such a slow movement in which the variations of the march theme are interwoven with a more song-like idea, helping to break up what would otherwise be a very repetitious piece.

Rondo

It is very rare to find a **rondo** anywhere other than in the last movement of a multi-movement work. The form is characterised by the alternation of a main theme – usually light in character and easily recognisable – with contrasting episodes. It is one of the easiest forms to understand and it was therefore conventionally found in the light, frothy final movement rather than the more serious first and second movements. If a symphony were a four-course meal, the rondo would be the dessert. It is a fun sort of movement because of the catchiness of its main thematic material and the regular tonic-key returns of that material. Rather like the chorus of a pop song, it proves to be very satisfying to the ear and acts as a reassuring agent as the symphony comes to a close.

EX. 5.2 HAYDN, SYMPHONY NO. 94 IN G, 'SURPRISE', IV, BARS 136–153 (RETRANSITION)

The main theme of a rondo will usually be set in rounded binary form. This is convenient because the theme will be neatly closed in its own key. It is also important because it already contains quite a lot of repetition, which makes subsequent returns of the theme very easy to recognise and anticipate. The contrasting episodes feature a change of theme and key which provide the dual effect of adding variety to the music while also delaying the next repetition of the theme, which would become rather dull if we were simply to hear it over and over again! Episodes sometimes contain clever or witty ways of returning to the rondo theme. Haydn was particularly successful with this strategy, and the linking passages between the ends of episodes and the return of the main theme are often very inventive, using the opening motivic idea of the theme as a sort of connective tissue at the end of the preceding episode (see **EX. 5.2**).

Having seen some of the contrasting strategies used in individual movements, it is important to consider how they are combined to create a unified work. The generic layout for the classical symphony could be described as a four-part journey consisting of a statement, reflection, return, and confirmation, with the four movements achieving these basic objectives. This, however, is only the most basic layout, and there have been many composers who have succeeded in varying, reinventing, or even revolutionising it.

The minor mode

One of the most important questions for composers is how to construct a coherent symphonic narrative when the work is in a minor key. The first movement would be in the tonic minor, which by convention is used to express negative emotions. In the eighteenth and nineteenth centuries the minor mode was a problem that needed to be struggled against. The slow movement would normally be in a related major key offering some relief from the tonic minor, and the Minuet movement would do the job of restoring the minor-mode condition established at the outset. The finale then, is crucial. Either it successfully escapes its minor-mode predicament and establishes a major-mode condition producing a positive, romantic, heroic, or comedic narrative, or it fails to do this and remains stuck tragically or stoically in the minor mode. Composers tended to have their preferred strategies in this regard. Haydn usually chose the more optimistic turn to the major mode at the end, whereas Mozart tended to stick to the more resigned minor.

In the nineteenth century, the heroic narrative of 'from darkness to light' became very common in minor-key works. This was apparent as early as Haydn's era but really took off after Beethoven's two minor-key symphonies, the Fifth and the Ninth, both of which chart heroic trajectories to the tonic major in their finales. This strategy became very common, to the point that ending a minor-key work in the minor mode was an exception to the rule. Clear examples of the darkness-to-light type strategy include:

- Schumann's Fourth in D minor
- Brahms's First in C minor
- Tchaikovsky's Fourth in F minor
- Tchaikovsky's Fifth in E minor
- Borodin's Second in B minor
- Saint-Saëns's Third in C minor

Alternatively, it was not unusual for composers to choose another option, including beginning the finale in the minor mode, saving the redemption to the major only until the end, and sometimes the very end: last-minute reversals of fortune in which the symphony snatches victory from the jaws of defeat can be very exciting! Such examples include:

- Mendelssohn's Third (the 'Scottish') in A minor
- Dvořák's Seventh in D minor
- Dvořák's Ninth ('From the New World') in E minor
- Bruckner's Eighth in C minor

Of course, the alternative is to end tragically, with the suggestion that the music itself has failed in its central task of escaping the minor mode, and remains in that emotionally charged state to the end. Instances of this tragic narrative are rarer but there are some important works including:

- Tchaikovsky's Sixth Symphony (the 'Pathétique'), ending in B minor
- Sibelius's First Symphony in E minor, featuring a tragic outpouring of emotion before an emptied-out close.
- Brahms's Fourth Symphony. Emotionally ambiguous and poker-faced, it ends unsentimentally in the tonic, E minor.

Symphonies that reverse the basic tonal narrative (i.e., which begin in the major mode but end in the minor) are extremely rare, and the fatalistic implications of 'light-to-darkness' would require some considerable reflection on the part of the listener in order to decipher the communicative intentions of the composer. That said, there is one work occupying a central place in the repertoire that does just this: Mendelssohn's Fourth Symphony (the 'Italian') in A major, whose finale plunges into A minor – a tonally strategic fall from which it never recovers.

Cyclical symphonies

In the early days of symphonic writing thematic, temporal, and tonal contrasts were unified within an overarching tonic. This was enough to provide a strong feeling of unity: each movement gave a sense that it belonged with the others and in a particular order. As symphonies became longer and more complex, the difficulty of maintaining unity became more of a challenge. One technique used to overcome this was to share thematic material across the different movements. This is sometimes obvious, with a movement directly quoting one or more previous movements. Sometimes it's rather more subtle, with the motivic content of one movement being employed later to produce apparently new material which is nevertheless related.

Beethoven's Fifth Symphony combines both methods, producing four sharply contrasting movements that nevertheless flow one into the next with an extremely strong sense of overarching unity. The four-note motive (**EX. 5.3A**) presented at the outset of the symphony is treated in an extremely intensive way throughout the first movement, appearing in almost every bar. The second movement offers some relief from this motive, but it returns in a new triple-metre guise, flattened out to a monotone, in the third movement (**EX. 5.3B**). By the time we're hit with the finale the motive has been transformed into an affirmational and optimistic presence which, while no longer the principle theme, accompanies the heroic fanfares that solidify C major and the escape from the minor mode (**EX. 5.3C**).

EX. 5.3A THE FOUR-NOTE MOTIVE IS INTRODUCED IN BEETHOVEN, SYMPHONY NO. 5 IN C MINOR, OP. 67, I, BARS 1–5

EX. 5.3B THE MONOTONE FOUR-NOTE MOTIVE APPEARS IN TRIPLE METRE IN BEETHOVEN, SYMPHONY NO. 5, III, BARS 19–26

After Beethoven, the strategy of sharing thematic material across the different movements of a symphony became much more common. The concept of the ***idée fixe*** is important for Berlioz's symphonies. In the cases of the *Symphonie Fantastique* and *Harold en Italie*, the music is unified by a common theme that is threaded throughout each movement. Sharing of melodic material did not always have to be organised like this, however, and there are two other important methods that were employed in the second half of the nineteenth century. The first of these was to follow what Beethoven had done in his Fifth Symphony and bring back the theme from the first movement in the finale. This has an important framing effect, with the theme signalling the beginning and the end of the musical narrative. This effect is strengthened when combined with the 'darkness-to-light' tonal strategy discussed above because the positive transfiguration of previously fatalistic minor-mode material can produce a powerfully heroic effect. Tchaikovsky's Fifth Symphony is a classic example in which the E minor introduction to the first movement is reconfigured to form the basis of the E major finale which romps triumphantly to victory.

The other important strategy that nineteenth-century composers employed to give a sense of unity was gradually to accumulate thematic material as the work proceeds, giving the impression that at each stage of the work the composer is bringing all the previous themes along too. **Dvořák's Ninth Symphony in E minor** ('From the New World') provides a clear model of this sort. The primary theme from the first movement is quoted at the climax of the second movement. The primary and secondary themes from the first movement are then quoted in the coda of the Scherzo. Themes from all three preceding movements are quoted, sometimes in counterpoint, in the finale, culminating in the movement's coda which superimposes the primary theme of the first movement and the primary theme of the finale (see **EX. 5.4**). Another legendary example of this technique can be found right at the end of Bruckner's Eighth Symphony in C minor, in which all of the main themes from the entire work are jammed together on the last page of the score, creating a dense mass of thematic material which brings the symphony to a resonant close.

Movement order, additions and elisions

The four-movement plan became the norm for the symphony in Vienna from about 1770. Before this time, symphonies could have either three movements (fast–slow–fast) or four (usually fast–slow–Minuet–fast). Occasionally we find works by Haydn and Mozart that go against the grain. In late-eighteenth-century France, three movements was the fashion, so Mozart omitted the Minuet from his Symphony No. 31 in D major, 'Paris'. The strongly expressed norm, however, was the pattern discussed above. By the time this tradition had solidified it became possible to play against it by altering the **order of the movements**. This usually applies to the middle movements – the first movement and the finale retained their roles as the 'book ends' of the work, whereas it became possible to switch the positioning of the inner movements so that the Minuet would be in second place, followed by the slow movement. This creates quite a pleasing effect because it is possible to follow the potentially very serious first movement with a relatively light-hearted Minuet, and then to have something more serious once again in the slow third movement.

in tempo (Allegro con fuoco)

This strategy is used in:

+ Mendelssohn's Third Symphony in A minor, the 'Scottish'
+ Borodin's First Symphony in E♭
+ Bruckner's Eighth Symphony in C minor
+ Mahler's First Symphony in D

During the nineteenth century the practice of **inserting extra movements** into the basic structure became more common. This was not normative even in the twentieth century, so whenever we find movements we're not expecting it should be registered as a surprising alteration to the expected plan. The most common way of doing this was to add a further slow movement between the Minuet and the finale. The classic example of this is Schumann's Third Symphony in E♭, the 'Rhenish', which contains a very unusual slow movement that uses the type of polyphonic writing more commonly found in sacred music. The idea here was to evoke the image of Cologne Cathedral, located on the banks of the River Rhine, which is the subject of the work. Tchaikovsky inserted a waltz (in effect, a slow Scherzo) between the first movement and the slow movement of his Third Symphony in D major. The 'real' Scherzo, when it does arrive in fourth place, is very unusual in that it is composed in $\frac{2}{4}$ time. So, it is as if the 'dance' aspect has already been ticked off the symphony's to-do list, freeing the Scherzo to express itself in an unconventional time signature.

Another strategy that became increasingly common from the middle of the nineteenth century was to **link some (or even all) of the movements together**. This may come as a surprise since the story of the symphony in the eighteenth century was largely about separating out the different movement types. Beethoven provided two models early in the century in his Fifth and Sixth Symphonies (premièred in the same concert in 1808), which in different ways make links between their later movements. In the case of his Sixth Symphony in F, the 'Pastoral', the Scherzo is 'interrupted' by the stormy fourth movement. After the storm, the finale emerges seamlessly as if the clouds have passed and the sun is coming back out again. This creates quite a long stretch of uninterrupted music unlike anything we find in Haydn or Mozart. In Beethoven's Fifth Symphony, the link at the end of the grittily determined C minor third movement is pivotal in terms of the escape from the minor mode. C major emerges triumphantly at the beginning of the finale, but the effect is significantly enhanced by the sense of anticipation generated by the A♭ transitional music which builds towards the explosive C major announcing the finale proper.

There were many attempts to join together all the movements to create one continuous work. The classic examples of this only came later, in the twentieth century, with Nielsen's Fourth Symphony (1916) and Sibelius's Seventh (1924). There is, however, one other important nineteenth-century example, namely Robert Schumann's Fourth Symphony in D minor, in which there are no breaks or gaps between any of the movements.

The works cited above represent interesting and creative exceptions to the general rule that symphonies between 1750 and 1900 nearly always contain four separate movements in a particular order. All but two of Beethoven's are normative in this respect, and all but one of Schubert's. There is no such exception in Dvořák's, or Brahms's output, who preferred to keep their movements separate and their movement-order traditional.

6
Sonata form

Sonata form was the most important and most fully developed form used for instrumental music in the late eighteenth and nineteenth centuries. It was habitually used as the basis for first movements of symphonies, sonatas, and chamber music during this time, and it is frequently found in slow movements and finales too. The most common version of this form, and the one we will concentrate on in this chapter, is organised into three sections: the **exposition**, the **development**, and the **recapitulation**. It was this plan that was developed in Mannheim and then solidified into a common practice in Vienna. Though it continued to change significantly through the nineteenth century, the symphonic first movements of Brahms, Tchaikovsky, and Bruckner retained these overarching units of formal organisation and are therefore comparable with the music of Stamitz, C.P.E. Bach, and Haydn.

Sonata form, like most musical forms, has both a tonal plot and a thematic plot. These two aspects are closely linked, and though it is possible to address each of them separately, it is crucial to understand how they relate. It is even possible to say that one of these aspects serves the other, though the relationship is not arranged in the way you might think. When analysing a piece in sonata form, the themes that we hear usually serve the purpose of achieving a tonal goal. In the same way that in a story the goal might be for the protagonist to find true love, the goal of the sonata's themes is to achieve closure in the tonic key. If it were simply to achieve this straightaway, however, it would make for a very short and banal story indeed and, as in a fairy tale, the sonata must go through several twists and turns, subplots, and deviations before it can properly achieve its goal. The word 'goal' here is crucial. All music in the tonal system should be understood as moving towards a goal (usually a cadence of some sort). This is what gives it the impression of having a beginning, a middle, and an end, and it's also why the idea of narrative – the way a piece of music is capable of telling a story – is so powerful in any discussion of this repertoire.

Exposition

The goal of the **exposition** is to achieve tonal closure in a key away from the tonic. The tonal goal is V if the piece is in the major mode, and III if the piece is minor. Tonal closure is achieved by establishing a perfect cadence in the new key, and the way in which this happens sets out the map for the whole movement. For instance, the dominant cadence at the end of the exposition is produced by the same material that produces the tonic cadence at the end of the whole movement. The exposition, then, moves from tonic to dominant (I–V) and this tonal motion is achieved by a series of themes.

The music has to begin in the tonic key with a **primary theme (P)** in order to provide a sense of tonal orientation. The cadence at the end of the exposition is achieved by a **secondary theme (S)**, that occurs in the dominant.[1] Therefore, we can say that the task of the secondary theme is to achieve a perfect cadence in its own key. The primary and secondary themes usually contrast in character. It is quite common for P to be loud, fanfare-like, or otherwise triadic, though quiet P themes are also possible. A unison statement at the beginning of P is a common classical strategy. By contrast, S is often quiet, lyrical, or songlike; it might be reflective in nature compared with the more declamatory P theme.

The primary theme (in the tonic) and secondary theme (in the dominant) do not merely succeed each other. This would create a tonal jolt, and so a passage of music is needed to connect the two themes together. Let's call this passage the **transition (TR)**. The transition will usually follow on from P and it is sometimes easily identifiable by a sudden change of texture and an increase in volume, scoring, and rhythmic activity. Alternatively, the primary theme can blend into the transition and the two can operate almost as if they are inseparable.

At the end of the exposition, after the dominant perfect cadence has been attained by the secondary theme, it is normal to find one or more ideas that confirm the arrival of the new key. This is called the **closing zone (C)**, though you might sometimes see it referred to as a **codetta**. This passage might contain some additional cadential activity and it frequently contains new material, though a reference to the primary theme at this point is not uncommon. The end of the closing zone is marked by a double bar with a repeat sign, and this also signals the end of the exposition. This succession of themes (P–TR–S–C) forms the basic plan for classical sonata expositions. The themes always appear in this order and each fulfils a particular tonal objective. We can therefore divide the exposition into two broad tonal parts, where P and TR establish the tonic key and then begin to move away from it, compared with S and C, which establish and confirm the dominant.

FIG. 6.1 SCHEMATIC DIAGRAM OF SONATA FORM EXPOSITION[2]

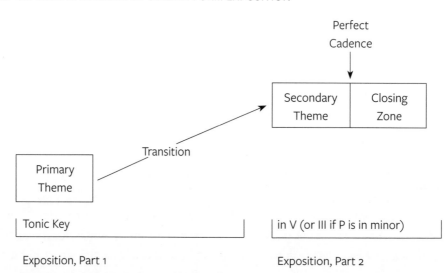

1   We use the terms set out in James Hepokoski and Warren Darcy, *Elements of Sonata Theory* (Oxford: Oxford University Press, 2006), when referring to sonata form.
2   Based on Hepokoski (2021), 54.

Development

The norm for first movements from about 1770 was for a **development section** to be inserted between the exposition and the recapitulation. The development section serves many purposes. As the name suggests, it develops the themes that we heard in the exposition, but it also leads to more distant tonal regions, getting away from the tonic–dominant polarity that we have heard until now. It is also the hardest part of sonata form to generalise about: unlike the exposition and recapitulation, where the conventions are quite strongly expressed in the repertoire, development sections offer much more freedom for the composer to decide what to do, and as a result there are many different ways of constructing them. The beginning and the end of the development, however, are the most straightforward parts to discuss in general terms.

Just as the exposition and the recapitulation have dual tasks to fulfil – tonal and thematic – so does the development. Its basic tonal objective is relatively clear: to reach the dominant as a chord. The strongest way of preparing any key is to go through its own dominant. Therefore, the strongest way to prepare the arrival of the tonic at the beginning of the recapitulation is to arrive at the dominant by the end of the development. The passage of music that achieves this task is called the **retransition**. Retransitions are usually organised by approaching the dominant and then standing on it for a protracted period of time by means of a **dominant pedal**. Once the development has arrived at this point – with the dominant harmony established as a chord rather than as a key in its own right – the return of P and the tonic (known as a 'double return') becomes an inevitability.

At the beginning of the development section, there is sometimes a short link that connects the end of the exposition to the development proper. This is followed by the first element of the section, which is known as a **preparation zone**. Here, composers usually begin with primary thematic material, however, there is often a decisive move to a different key. Sometimes composers begin their development sections in the dominant (where the exposition left off), but it's quite common to find more distant tonal relationships, which include the dominant minor, mediant, or submediant relationships.

Composers use the heart of the development section, let's call it the **central action**, to break down the different parts of the primary theme into smaller components and then reorganise them in new and exciting combinations. The most common methods of doing this include musical devices such as:

- imitation
- fragmentation
- sequential and modulatory motion
- counterpoint
- fugue

The central action usually builds up in terms of dynamics, texture, and rhythmic intensity towards a climax, and this is why it is nearly always the strident primary and transitional thematic material that is used here and not the calmer and more reflective secondary theme. The entire development section in the first movement of Haydn's 'London' Symphony, No. 104, for example, is built on a single six-note idea drawn from the middle of the P theme (first heard in bars 19–20). This is also the point of greatest tension in the movement, and composers tend to position this moment just before the retransition, at which point the tension is harnessed by the dominant pedal and then discharged into the double return of theme and key, kick-starting the recapitulation. The first movement of **Mozart's Symphony No. 38 in D, 'Prague'**, contains a typical (and very beautiful) example of this (**EX. 6.1**). Notice how the bass arrives at the dominant in bar 187 and then, aside from the brief German augmented sixth in bar 196, the dominant remains in place in the horns and basses until the start of the recapitulation in bar 208. During this time the other instruments play contrapuntally above the dominant in the bass, but this really only serves to prolong the dominant retransition over a longer period of time and not to move anywhere else harmonically. The effect of this prolonged dominant pedal at the bottom of the texture is to prepare and dramatise the return of the tonic at the beginning of the recapitulation.

Recapitulation

Where the exposition provides a plan for tonal closure by achieving a perfect cadence in a different key – normally the dominant – the **recapitulation** employs that plan to achieve closure in the tonic. In doing this, it fulfils the central task of sonata form: to secure its key with a perfect cadence. It is therefore normal to hear all of the material from the exposition again in the recapitulation, which follows the basic plan outlined above: P–TR–S–C. In eighteenth-century sonata forms the recapitulation is considered to generate a 'structure of accomplishment' in response to the 'structure of promise' that we find in the exposition.[3] It is therefore logical to discuss the recapitulation in relation to the exposition.

The main difference between the exposition and the recapitulation is tonal. Whereas the primary theme in both cases is heard in the tonic, the secondary theme and any closing material heard in the dominant in the exposition is now heard in the tonic as well. Sometimes this involves only the necessary transposition down a fifth, though some composers preferred to vary the material by changing the texture, extending or abbreviating the material, or sometimes by adding a countermelody. Mozart typically preferred to keep the exposition and the recapitulation very similar in profile, only making the necessary changes to stop the music from modulating away from the tonic. This has the effect of producing a classical balance and symmetry between the exposition and recapitulation. Haydn, by contrast, saw the recapitulation as an opportunity to show off how much he could do to reinvent his musical materials. In the recapitulation of the first movement of his 'Military' Symphony, No. 100 in G, for example, Haydn rushes through much of the primary and secondary material in a matter of a few bars (the transition does not appear at all here), and then radically expands the final stages of the secondary material, continuing to develop it even as the movement is coming to a close.[4]

The beginning of the recapitulation is usually quite easy to identify because it normally begins with a statement of the primary theme in the tonic key (a 'double return'). In the nineteenth century the beginning of the recapitulation was a moment of dramatic arrival and re-beginning,

---

3   Hepokoski and Darcy, *Elements of Sonata Theory*.
4   See Hepokoski's analysis in *A Sonata Theory Handbook*, 86–104.

EX. 6.1 MOZART, SYMPHONY NO. 38 IN D, 'PRAGUE', I, BARS 187–212

Recapitulation

and many composers increased the intensity of scoring, dynamics, and register at this point in order to emphasise its importance in the musical narrative. The recapitulation in the first movement of Beethoven's First Symphony in C major is a clear example of this.

The secondary theme and the closing zone would normally remain relatively unchanged in the recapitulation, save for the necessary transposition to the tonic key. Likewise, the primary theme could appear as before, or in an intensified version. The transition in the recapitulation would usually have to undergo some significant changes, however. This is because it falls to the transition to perform the modulation to the dominant in the exposition, and in the recapitulation this modulation has to be eradicated. There are several strategies that composers used to solve this compositional puzzle in the late eighteenth century. A favourite of **Mozart**'s was quickly to introduce a subdominant flavour after the onset of P. In his **Symphony No. 31 in D, 'Paris'**, for example, Mozart introduces a C♮ in the bass at this point (suggesting the subdominant, G major) which acts as an antidote to the habit of modulating to the dominant: tonally speaking, the music is moving in the opposite (flatward) direction and not in the sharpward direction of the dominant (see **EX. 6.2**).

In Mozart's and Haydn's symphonies we frequently encounter quite a large amount of recomposition soon after the beginning of the recapitulation, somewhere in the P→TR zone. When this happens, there is usually a moment when the music snaps back into correspondence with the exposition, typically a fifth lower or a fourth higher, in order to prepare the secondary theme in the tonic. It is the secondary theme, then, which produces the perfect cadence that secures the tonic key and closes the form.

First-movement sonata forms with exposition, development, and recapitulation were the most common option from around 1770 until the end of the nineteenth century. **FIG. 6.2** shows the schematic layout of this form.

FIG. 6.2 SCHEMATIC DIAGRAM OF SONATA FORM[5]

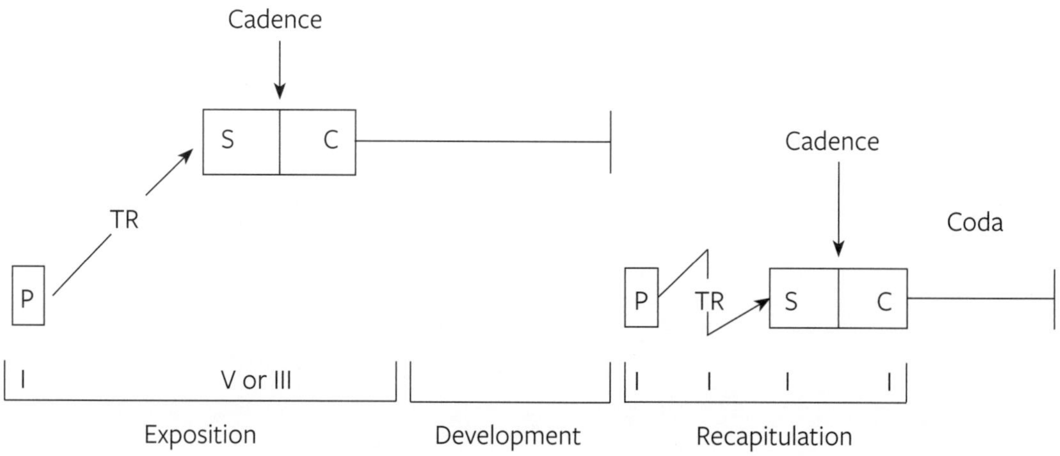

Key: (P) primary theme   (S) secondary theme   (TR) transition   (C) closing zone

---

5   Based on Hepokoski (2021), 54.

Introductions and codas

It is normal for the first movement of a symphony to consist only of an exposition, a development, and a recapitulation; however, as the symphony developed in the eighteenth century, composers began to add 'framing functions' to their sonata forms. These are not part of the form as such, but exist outside of it like bookends to the main action of the movement.

The most common of these framing functions is the **coda**, which appears after the end of the recapitulation. The purpose of a coda is to add further weight to the tonal resolution of the recapitulation. Codas can vary in length. In the most basic cases the coda might simply provide some further cadential confirmation, however, it is possible for codas to be rather more lengthy, sometimes continuing the argument of the sonata form. Cases of this sort can be found quite readily in Haydn's and Mozart's music, but it was Beethoven who really began the tradition of the coda as a fully fledged section of a first movement. It is usually possible to identify the beginning of the coda by a change of texture, dynamics, and orchestration, and by observing how the end of the exposition compares with the end of the recapitulation. The first movement of Beethoven's Third Symphony is an important example of a discursive coda that continues to develop the material even after the tonic has been secured in the recapitulation – it is almost like Beethoven composed a further development section, as if the music had more to say and needed to spill over the normal limits of the form.

If the coda is considered to come 'after the end' of the sonata form, then the **introduction** can be said to come 'before the beginning'. Again, introductions are not necessary in all cases, and there are many symphonic first movements that do perfectly well without them. When they do occur, they tend to be in a slower tempo than the rest of the movement, which can produce a sense of grandeur. Imagine an oil painting with a big, ornate, gold frame – it's that sort of grand effect that a slow introduction achieves in music. Introductions also have a tonal role to play. While they nearly always begin in the tonic, they usually arrive on dominant harmony just before the start of the exposition. This produces an elegant preparation for the main body of the movement.

Although Mozart did compose introductions to his first-movement sonata forms (e.g., Symphonies No. 36 in C, 'Linz', No. 38 in D, 'Prague', and No. 39 in E♭), it was Haydn who pioneered the technique and perfected it in his 'London' Symphonies – a collection of 12 works which he composed between 1791 and 1795. Of these 12 symphonies, only one (No. 95 in C minor) does not feature a slow introduction, suggesting that Haydn increasingly considered it to be a necessary part of the form for large-scale works. Note also that it is usually the first movement that receives an introduction and not any of the following movements, since the introduction serves not only to lay the foundations for that movement, but for the symphony as a whole.

By the 1790s, introductions were already quite common. This allowed composers to experiment with them. **Haydn's Symphony No. 104, 'London',** is in D major; however, when we hear the first notes of the introduction, which consist only of tonic and dominant, it is impossible to tell whether the music is major or minor. It is only in bar 3, when we hear the F♮ in the bass of a first-inversion chord of D minor that the mode of the music becomes apparent (see **EX. 6.3**). Of course, when we reach the sonata form proper at the start of the exposition, the shadow

EX. 6.3 HAYDN, SYMPHONY NO. 104, 'LONDON', I, BARS 1–4

is lifted as the primary theme is played in a sunny D major, but the slow D minor introduction gives a sense of weight and seriousness to the work as a whole.

Only a few years later in 1800, Beethoven had finished composing his First Symphony in C, which also contains an introduction to its first movement. This is a fascinating example because instead of strongly establishing the tonic (as Haydn did with his emphatic references to I and V), Beethoven actively avoids establishing tonic harmony, saving its arrival until the start of the exposition. This creates a sense of suspense and anticipation. Beethoven begins his introduction on a chord of C major, but it contains a dissonance, a B♭, making it sound like the dominant of F rather than the tonic of the piece. This motion is confirmed with a move to F major. Beethoven then suggests a motion to C through its own dominant, G, but this is deflected to A minor. Then, the music moves to G major, the dominant, where we are presented with a lyrical introductory theme. The dominant provides the harmonic basis for the rest of the introduction and the first time C major is fully established is at the change of tempo as the primary theme of the exposition is played.

CASE STUDY: SYMPHONY NO. 1 IN G (1779) BY JOSEPH BOLOGNE, CHEVALIER DE SAINT-GEORGES

Let's look now at an example of a symphonic first movement. This symphony was composed in Paris in the late 1770s and it has many typical characteristics of classical form. The movement is in sonata form and it contains an exposition, a development section, and a recapitulation. While it is an exciting and dynamic piece of music, it is also relatively light-hearted in mood. This may have led the composer to think that a slow introduction was not necessary. Likewise, at the end of the movement there is a small amount of extra confirmation of the tonic, but nothing that could be described as a coda.

EXPOSITION (bars 1–105)

Primary theme (1–31): This establishes the tonic, G major, as well as the energetic and playful mood of the movement. Notice that there is more than one idea here. We have the arpeggiated melody at the beginning, and then a syncopated idea beginning at bar 9. There is yet another idea at bar 17, before a return to the opening arpeggiated idea at bar 24. All of these ideas are in the tonic key, so they all belong to the primary thematic area.

Transition (32–49): We can identify this by the sudden change of texture and dynamics. The horns and oboes begin to play in a much more sustained way, and the music moves very suddenly from *piano* to *forte*. There are still some remnants of the primary theme in the cellos, basses, and violas, but the change of tonal direction by the addition of C♯s at bar 41 confirms that the music is in the transition section. Notice how the textural and rhythmic energy builds to a climax at bar 48, arriving on a chord of A major which is the dominant of the next tonal area of the piece.

Secondary theme (50–65): This can be identified by the sudden drop in texture and dynamics, and by the presentation of the dominant, D major, as an established key. The secondary theme is more lyrical and song-like than the primary theme. Notice how it mainly moves in a step-wise fashion, compared with the primary theme, which contained lots of leaps. The theme is structured as a period, containing an antecedent phrase (50–57) which arrives on a local dominant chord of A major, and a consequent phrase (58–65) which produces a perfect cadence in D major. This does the job of firmly securing the main structural goal of the exposition, to achieve a perfect cadence in the new key. Anything that comes after this moment must therefore belong to the closing zone.

Closing zone (66–105): Now that the new key of D major is completely secure, Bologne confirms the key with a closing zone. In this case, the closing zone falls into two phases. The first (66–89) provides a playful preparation for the flourish to come at the end of the exposition. Notice how the music descends via a sequence to establish the local dominant (a chord of A major) at bar 74, which the composer then builds up with a *crescendo*. This prepares the virtuosic second phase of the closing zone (90–105) which puts the new key of D major beyond any doubt. At this point we arrive at a double bar with dots, which indicates that we have reached the end of the exposition section and it will now be repeated.

DEVELOPMENT (bars 106–165)

Preparation zone (106–125): The music 'starts again' here. There is no linking passage. We simply hear the primary theme in its original presentation (i.e., not broken down into its smaller parts yet), but in the dominant, D major. So, tonally speaking, the development starts where the exposition left off. After eight bars of D major, the tonality begins to destabilise. At bar 114 a descending sequence is set up, based on a motif from the secondary theme. The tonal destination of this passage is the relative minor (vi).

Central action (126–151): This is the most tonally unstable passage in the movement. The music arrives in E minor at this point, which is the first time we have heard a sustained period in the minor mode. The main motive from the primary theme can be heard in the basses, cellos, and violas, driving the music forward. Primary thematic material continues to dominate in the syncopated music that follows, and the goal of this passage is to reach the home dominant, D major, but as a chord rather than as a key.

Retransition (152–165): At the start of the development, D major behaved as an established key in its own right. Here, however, D behaves as a chord – V of G major – which needs to resolve. The retransition can be easily identified by the dominant pedal in the cellos, basses, and horns (remember, the horn is a transposing instrument, so the written G in the horn part will sound a fourth lower!). This is typical. A long dominant note at the bottom of the texture is a common technique used to prepare the return of the tonic key. Notice that there is quite a bit of contrapuntal activity in the upper voices, including some sequential motion as well as a reference to the tonic minor with the introduction of B♭s. The suggestion of the minor mode at this point adds to the drama because it raises a question over whether the music really will

TABLE 6.1 SCHEMATIC DESIGN OF JOSEPH BOLOGNE, CHEVALIER DE SAINT-GEORGES'
SYMPHONY NO. 1 IN G (1779), ALLEGRO

'Allegro' from Symphony No. 1 in G (1779) by Joseph Bologne, Chevalier de Saint-Georges				
Exposition (bars 1–105)	**Primary theme** (1–31)	**Transition** (32–49)	**Secondary theme** (50–65)	**Closing zone** (66–105)
	◆ Establishes tonic of G major ◆ Several melodic ideas all in the tonic	◆ Sudden change of texture and dynamics ◆ Change of tonal direction ◆ Textural and rhythmic energy builds up to chord V of the next tonal area of the piece	◆ Sudden drop in texture and dynamics ◆ The dominant, D major, established as the key ◆ More lyrical and song-like than P ◆ Structural goal of exposition is achieved: cadence in a new key	◆ New key of D major is secured and confirmed
Development (bars 106–165)	**Preparation zone** (106–125)		**Central action** (126–151)	**Retransition** (152–165)
	◆ Music 'starts again', without a linking passage, but in the dominant ◆ The tonal destination of this passage is the relative minor (vi)		◆ Tonally unstable ◆ Music arrives in E minor, which is the first time we have heard a sustained period in the minor mode ◆ Primary material continues to dominate ◆ The goal of this passage is to reach the home dominant, D major, but as a chord rather than as a key	◆ D now behaves as a chord (V of G major) which needs to resolve ◆ Retransition is identified by the dominant pedal
Recapitulation (bars 166–247)	**Primary theme** (166–189)	**Transition** (—)	**Secondary theme** (190–205)	**Closing zone** (206–247)
	◆ Music 'starts again' with the primary theme in the tonic	◆ The music at the start of the recapitulation is already in the tonic, so there's no need for any transition	◆ Now in the tonic key, the secondary theme follows directly and achieves a perfect cadence in the tonic	◆ Closing materials are cycled through as before, adding further weight and solidity to G major ◆ An extra two bars are added at the end to signal the close of the movement

recover G major again. This is the darkest moment in the narrative of the movement, and the point of greatest tension.

RECAPITULATION (bars 166–247)

Primary theme (166–189): After the long dominant retransition, the music 'starts again' once more with the primary theme in the tonic. The double-return of theme and key signals the beginning of the recapitulation. The next question is how the composer will change things in order to avoid moving away from the tonic...

Transition (—): The music at the beginning of the recapitulation is already in the tonic, so there is no need for any transition at all – Bologne simply omits this passage! It is an unusual decision, but an effective one.

Secondary theme (190–205): Now in the tonic key, the secondary theme follows directly and achieves the central goal of the form – to secure a perfect cadence in the tonic, G major. This happens in bars 205–206.

Closing zone (206–247): With the tonic key secure, the closing materials are cycled through as before, adding further weight and solidity to G major. An extra two bars of emphatic G major are added at the end to signal the close of the movement.

◆   ◆   ◆

Different types of sonata form

The form outlined above, with exposition, development, recapitulation, and optional introduction and coda, was the most common way of composing the first movement of a symphony from about 1770 until the middle of the nineteenth century (around the time of Mendelssohn and Schumann). It was not the only way, however. Before 1770 there were many different ways of organising the first movement of a symphony. We can still recognise these as examples of sonata form, but there was much less uniformity of approach among early symphonists such as Stamitz, Wagenseil, J. C. Bach, and Sammartini. It was quite common in these early years for sonata forms not to contain a development, for example. Sometimes the recapitulation would begin not with the primary theme, but with the transition or the secondary theme.

◆   ◆   ◆

It is important to stress that there was a diverse practice in European symphonic composition, and that a focus on a small number of figures working in the orbit of Vienna between about 1770 and 1810 tells only part of the story. Similarly, after about 1850, approaches to large-scale symphonic form became increasingly varied and this was largely a result of the experimentation with a more expansive tonal palette. This is the topic of the next chapter.

7
Tonality

The idea of tonal unity

Unity is one of the central characteristics of music from the tonal era. The idea of **tonal unity** can be seen in European repertoires from at least as early as the seventeenth century in the music of Purcell, Lully, Schütz, and Corelli. The main idea behind the concept of unity is that a given piece of music is governed by an overarching tonic, which acts as a point of reference to which everything else is related. Pieces of tonal music therefore tend to begin and end in the tonic, and visit related keys in the middle. This happens at different levels of magnification too. A large work like a symphony would, in the eighteenth century, begin and end in the tonic, but it would be common for 'inner' movements, usually the slow movement, to be set in a related key away from the tonic. Focusing in on that one movement, we would see a similar pattern: it would begin and end in the same key and visit related keys in the middle. In this sense, much like a snowflake, tonal music is organised in the same way at different levels of magnification.

Tonality itself, however, is notoriously difficult to define. It is relatively simple to describe what it does and how it works but defining *what it is* has stumped music theorists for centuries. Even now, tonality can be hard to describe, and we quickly end up using technical terminology (such as Roman numerals) or resorting to metaphors as we have been throughout this book. Talk of 'tonal goals' is a common metaphor, as well as the music 'moving' from one key to another: the music doesn't 'move' anywhere at all in a literal sense – it's just sound!

It is possible, however, to discuss certain conventions that we can hear in the repertoire of tonal music, and in the eighteenth- and nineteenth-century symphony in particular. In general terms, the story of tonality from 1750 until 1900 is a story of ever-increasing complexity, a story about the development from relatively straightforward triadic music towards a more complex chromatic palette. The development of tonal practice during this era ultimately led some composers to stretch the system to breaking point. Only a few years after 1900, Schoenberg and his students, who worked and composed in Vienna, had already developed a method of composition that was not reliant on conventional tonality, though, obviously tonality continues to enjoy a place in concert music as well as popular genres to this day. In this chapter we will consider some of the defining characteristics of classical tonality and 'tonal space', and examine some examples of how it developed after 1800.

Classical tonality: tonic, dominant, and harmonic tension

In the classical symphony, the tonic and dominant key areas are the structural pillars that individual movements and whole works are built on. We saw in Chapter 5 how all sorts of different musical forms are essentially structured around motion from tonic to dominant, and then a return to the tonic. In Chapter 6 we saw how the most complex musical form of the classical and romantic periods – sonata form – is built on the polarisation of tonic and dominant, which are articulated by the two contrasting themes. This polarisation is later resolved by cycling through the themes once again in the recapitulation, but with all the material in the tonic. It is possible to say, then, that the relationship between V and I in the classical style (and not the themes themselves) is the overriding driver of musical form. To make this clear, let's look at an example by Haydn that has already been discussed briefly in the previous chapter.

CASE STUDY: SYMPHONY NO. 104 IN D MAJOR, 'LONDON' (1795) BY JOSEPH HAYDN – FIRST MOVEMENT EXPOSITION

EXPOSITION: bars 17–123

Primary theme (17–31): This is organised as a period consisting of an antecedent phrase arriving on V at bar 24, and a consequent phrase confirming the tonic with a cadence in bars 31–32.

Transition (32–64): This is easily identifiable by the sudden change of texture (from strings only to full orchestral tutti), dynamics (from *piano* to *fortissimo*) and some new thematic material. Transitions fulfil two functions. The first is thematic – they mark the end of the primary theme and set up the secondary theme. The second is tonal, they usually modulate from tonic to dominant. Here these two jobs are treated separately. The transition begins in bar 32 with a marked change in texture, dynamics, and thematic material, but the harmonic motion away from the tonic does not begin until bar 50. It is in this passage that G♯s are introduced, signalling a modulation to A major. This modulation is confirmed at the end of the transition (bars 57–64) with the emphatic arrival on a chord of E major, which is chord V of the new key, A major.

Secondary theme (65–98): This is a quirk of Haydn's style: rather than composing a new theme at this point, he simply reuses the primary theme again! This strategy is known as **monothematicism**; Haydn uses the primary theme in the dominant in the second half of the exposition. This secondary thematic area can be divided into two components. First, there is the original melody, slightly varied from its earlier presentation (65–79). The major difference here is that, although it is once again presented as a musical period, it does not achieve a full cadence at the end because the bass in bar 80 lands not on A but on F♯. This is not enough to provide closure to the theme, and the material continues to spin out over a further 19 bars. This *Fortspinnung* passage comprises the second component of the secondary thematic area, which achieves closure with a perfect cadence in A major in bars 98–99.

Closing zone (99–123): This passage is tonally secure after the very strong cadence that lands in bar 99. The music provides ever stronger confirmation of this cadence, as is typical in the classical style.

TABLE 7.1 HAYDN, SYMPHONY NO. 104 IN D MAJOR, EXPOSITION

Haydn, Symphony No. 104 in D major, first movement				
Exposition (bars 17–123)	Primary theme (17–31)	Transition (32–64)	Secondary theme (65–98)	Closing zone (99–123)
	• A musical period establishing the tonic	• Increase in dynamic and textural intensity • Establishes V of the new key	• Establishes the dominant key area (A major) using material borrowed from the primary theme • Produces a perfect cadence in A major	• Further confirmation of A major

Monothematic expositions are commonplace in Haydn's symphonies. They are a demonstration of his inventiveness as a composer and his willingness to reuse and recycle old material, really squeezing as much as possible out of his themes. This technique also shows that the tonal tension between tonic and dominant is the main structural factor in organising a classical sonata form and not the contrast between the themes themselves, which is of only secondary importance. This began to change in the nineteenth century as the clarity of the tonic–dominant relationship began to break down and the content of the themes gradually became more important.

◆　◆　◆

Mapping tonal space

We cannot see tonality and it is therefore a difficult thing to measure. One useful way of getting around this problem is to imagine that the keys are arranged in spatial relation to each other on a map. Once we have worked out a way to do this it becomes possible to measure the 'distance' between keys and to construct a map of tonal space. One of the most common ways of mapping tonal space is to arrange the keys into a circle, otherwise known as the **circle of fifths**. A given tonal centre is located next to its most closely related keys (dominant, subdominant, and relative) which results in an outer circle of major keys and an inner circle of minor keys. The pattern this produces is a series of perfect fifths moving upwards in a clockwise direction and downwards moving anticlockwise (**FIG 7.1**). This gives a 'sharp side' on the right and a 'flat side' on the left. The area at the bottom of the circle is the 'enharmonic seam', where pitches can be notated either as sharps or flats. This is rather like the point on a world map where Russia and Alaska meet; on a flat surface they appear far apart, but on a globe they are next to each other.

The same is true for tonality: F♯ major (which contains six sharps) and D♭ major (five flats) may seem distant to look at on the page, but they are actually related by a tonic–dominant relationship. We can use the circle of fifths to measure not only the distance between keys in theory, but also the distances between keys in actual pieces of music. As you listen to the music described below, try mapping out which keys are visited on the circle of fifths. In the classical period it would have been unusual to venture far from the tonic, although examples do exist.

FIG. 7.1 CIRCLE OF FIFTHS

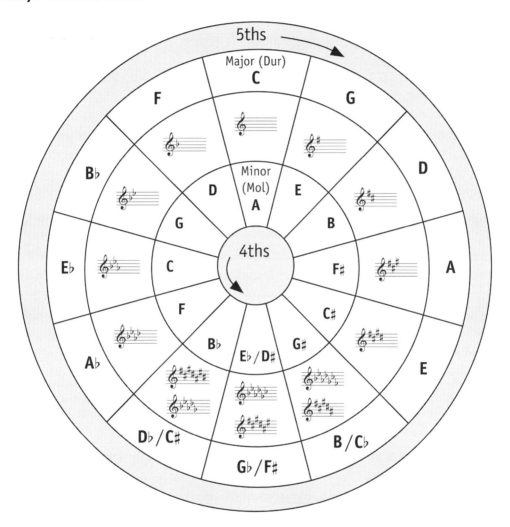

Beethoven and tonal antagonism

Examples of a breaking down of the tonic–dominant polarisation began to emerge ever more frequently after 1800. There are many examples in Beethoven's symphonies of an emphasis on more distant tonal relationships, and these examples often have to do with the concept of **tonal antagonism**, that is, there is something in the thematic content of the music that is antagonistic to the normal classical functioning of the form.

CASE STUDY: SYMPHONY NO. 1 IN C (1800) BY LUDWIG VAN BEETHOVEN – THIRD MOVEMENT

TABLE 7.2 BEETHOVEN'S SYMPHONY NO. 1 IN C MAJOR, MENUETTO

Beethoven, Symphony No. 1 in C major, third movement			
Minuet	**a** (1–8)	**b** (8–44)	**a′** (45–79)
	◆ A musical sentence establishing motion from tonic to dominant	◆ Increase in dynamic and textural intensity ◆ Motion to D♭ major (♭ II of C!)	◆ Recovery and confirmation of C major

The third movement, a Minuet in name only, is a clear example of a tonal antagonism being worked out in a very short space of time. The initial motion from tonic to dominant occurs in the first eight bars, which pass in a matter of seconds as the music effortlessly achieves its first goal of moving from I to V. After the double bar something slightly sinister happens: an A♭ is introduced, which temporarily suggests E♭ major. However, the flatward motion does not stop there. Soon we hear D♭s and G♭s being added and we quickly discover that the music settles in D♭ major, which is confirmed with a perfect cadence in bar 25. This is an enormous tonal distance to have travelled. D♭ major is the **Neapolitan** of C major (the flattened supertonic, a semitone above C). Many composers had been using the Neapolitan as a chord during the late baroque and classical periods, but it was a bold decision to use it as a key in the way Beethoven does here. The Neapolitan is one of the most distant keys from the tonic. Although it is only a half-step away in terms of the scale, it is a very long distance in harmonic terms if we look at the circle of fifths.

The problem at this point is how to initiate a retransition and recover C major again. This is achieved in a particularly vulgar way: the music simply moves up by a semitone at a time from B♭ at bar 35 until C is reached, and then the opening thematic material (the a′ section of the rounded binary form) is heard once again in C major, this time remaining in the tonic and cadencing in that key at bar 58. The music is not over, however, because D♭ still has something to say. In bars 58–65 the D♭ continues to antagonise the smooth functioning of C major. It is almost as if it is interrupting from outside of the key, and alternates with D♮ (which belongs to C major) like two characters jostling for position.

◆ ◆ ◆

Another example of such tonal antagonism can be heard in the finale of **Beethoven's Eighth Symphony in F**. This is a very strange movement. It sounds like it might be a rondo because we hear the primary theme in the tonic so many times, but it is actually in sonata form. Further to this, the form comes to an end about halfway through the movement, and the rest of the piece is coda (beginning at bar 273 and lasting until the end of the movement at bar 502!).

EX. 7.1 F♯ MINOR THEME IN BEETHOVEN, SYMPHONY NO. 8 IN D, OP. 93, IV, BARS 386–394

It is during this long and discursive coda that we hear the primary theme away from the tonic for the first time. This is an extremely disruptive gesture. The coda of a finale would ordinarily give a sense of tonal security, so anything away from the tonic at this point would be an unbalancing strategy. This is made even more unbalanced by Beethoven's choice of key. At bar 380 Beethoven chooses to present the theme in F♯ minor (**EX. 7.1**). So, there is a change of tonal centre to a remote key, a change of key signature to two sharps, and a change of mode from major to minor. The music circles around F♯ for several bars (making clever use of the galant 'Fenaroli' schema in a context that would barely have been imaginable in the music of J. C. Bach or the young Mozart, see Chapter 2) before the tonally antagonistic choice of key is violently 'corrected' with the introduction of the brass and timpani at bar 391, accompanied by the recovery of the original key signature. Such tonal antagonism was nascent in late-eighteenth-century music – there are examples to be found in many of Haydn's symphonies, for example – but it was Beethoven who intensified this approach to tonality, staging a 'problem' near the beginning of a large-scale work, in this case the deliberate 'wrong note' in bar 17, and then using tonality to violently 'correct' that problem. This is one of the tonal strategies that makes Beethoven's music so dramatic.

Schubert and tonal escapism

Beethoven began to experiment with expanding the tonal possibilities in his symphonies from around 1800 by exploring more distantly related keys and exploiting the inherent tension between those keys. He typically organised these tonal tensions by expressing them as a problem to be solved or an obstacle to overcome, before violently and noisily resolving those tensions. This was not the only way, though. In the second and third decades of the nineteenth century Schubert was also composing in Vienna, and although he has traditionally been viewed as a composer of songs (which number in the hundreds), he also wrote instrumental music, including piano sonatas, chamber music, and nine symphonies.

Like Beethoven, Schubert experimented with distant tonal regions in his music. Unlike Beethoven, however, he did not treat such distant tonal areas as an arena for violence or humour, but as a form of musical escapism. Distant tonal regions for Schubert are frequently the places where the music is in its most relaxed state, and these are often paired with lyrical or dreamy music that feels as if it could exist in a separate world from the rest of the piece. Let's look at some examples.

Schubert's Eighth Symphony is in B minor. It contains only two movements, and both of these feature some unusual tonal adventures. The first movement's sonata form features a particularly dark and edgy primary theme. The transition does not modulate and instead closes very firmly still in the tonic. This is unusual enough – normally the transition would modulate – but next, after the transition seems to have come to an end, two bassoons and two horns slip chromatically into the new key. Normally this would be the relative major (III), but in this case Schubert chooses G major (VI). At this point all the tension and angst that seemed to infuse the primary theme melts away as the music escapes into a new tonal world for the secondary theme.

EX. 7.2 SCHUBERT, SYMPHONY NO. 8 IN B MINOR, II, BARS 281–301

The themes in the slow movement of this symphony contain a similar sense of opposition; however, here it is the primary theme in E major that contains the dreamy and lyrical material and the secondary theme, which first appears in C♯ minor, expresses the more 'angsty' and nervous ideas. The most chromatically intense moment in the piece, however, is also the quietest. Towards the end of the movement (bar 281) the music moves between E major and A♭ major (up a major third, where A♭ is the enharmonic equivalent of G♯) through a chain of unaccompanied thirds in the violins, creating an extremely chromatically intense but also very delicate conclusion to the work (**EX. 7.2**).

In the first movement of Schubert's Sixth Symphony in C major, the motion from I to V for the secondary theme is achieved in the normal way. What happens within the secondary theme is more unusual, though. Unlike the kind of classical syntax that we saw in Chapter 4, in which themes were organised into sentences and periods that outlined a particular key, here the music does not want to settle. Although it begins as expected in G major in bar 79, by bar 94 the theme seems to have modulated up through a minor third and cadenced in B♭ major. This theme eventually does return to the dominant with a cadence at the end of the exposition, but the internal meanderings give a sense of tonal freedom in the music.

Two romantic harmonists: Dvořák and Bruckner

By the second half of the nineteenth century a much wider palette of tonal colours was available. This was down to at least two reasons. First, much of the groundwork for tonal experimentation had already been laid in the early part of the century by composers such as Beethoven, Schubert, Schumann, and Mendelssohn. Secondly, there had been an upheaval of the genre of the symphony, with the traditions that had been inherited from Haydn and Mozart being challenged by a new and progressive group of composers that included Berlioz, Liszt, and especially Wagner, whose near reinvention of the harmonic system sent shockwaves across European composition in the middle of the century. Many symphonists who were composing in the later nineteenth century, therefore, can be found experimenting with tonality in their music in a much more sustained and exploratory way. A quick example from **Dvořák's Ninth Symphony, 'From the New World'**, is enough to demonstrate this.

The choice of key for the slow movement is already highly unusual. The symphony is in E minor, but Dvořák chooses D♭ for this movement. This is the enharmonic equivalent of C♯ major (VI of E minor), but Dvořák notates the music in D♭ because it is much easier to read in five flats than it is in seven sharps! The catch here is that it begins in E – the old key from the preceding movement. The six-bar introduction, then, performs the task of modulating from the old key of the first movement to the new key of the slow movement (**EX. 7.3**). This motion looks just as astonishing as it sounds because it involves crossing the **enharmonic seam** – that is, it involves changing suddenly from notation in sharps (from where the music begins in E major) into flats (where the famous theme in D♭ major begins in bar 7). At this point, the fourth horn is still playing a G♯, even though the violas and the first trombone are playing A♭.

At the structural level, we can see how Dvořák's approach to tonality had the effect of dissolving the clear lines of distinction between tonic and dominant that were so crucial for the classical symphony. In the first movement of his Eighth Symphony (after an introduction

EX. 7.3 MOVEMENT ACROSS THE ENHARMONIC SEAM IN DVOŘÁK, SYMPHONY NO. 9 IN E MINOR, OP. 95, II, BARS 1–6

in G minor) the exposition moves from G major to B major. In this case the motion from I to V seems to have been replaced with motion from I to III. There is the added aspect that the secondary theme is presented in B minor (iii), with the further effect of smoothing over the change of key. (Motion from G major directly to B major is a jolt, whereas B minor is directly related to G major and it works as a convenient staging post for a later change of mode to B major.) It is as if Dvořák has imported a strategy from the minor mode and used it in a major-mode work.

Bruckner was strongly influenced by Wagner, and this influence can be heard quite clearly in his use of tonality. In Bruckner's music, cadences become much rarer, and this has a number of effects. Firstly, large spans of music unfold without the reassuring finality that cadences provide, leading to a much more continuous and exploratory effect. It can sometimes be difficult to pinpoint where one section ends and another begins. A lack of cadential articulation also means that lots of keys can be cycled through without ever being confirmed, and this is something that Bruckner experiments with in many of his themes. Let's look at the secondary theme from the finale of **Bruckner's Seventh Symphony in E major** (EX. 7.4). Here we can see that the theme begins in A♭ major, the enharmonic equivalent of III – already an unusual choice, at least by classical standards. To add further confusion to this moment, it is set up at the end of the transition not by its own dominant, but the dominant of F major, resulting in an unexpected harmonic turn when we hear A♭ and not F. As the theme progresses it becomes very clear that it is not going to outline a key in the conventional sense. It quickly moves from A♭ in bar 35 to B♭ minor in bar 38. Bars 39–42 make the same move, up a tone, but from B major to C♯ minor. It is unclear by this point exactly how A♭ major might be recovered, but Bruckner seems happy to carry on exploring where the theme might go and at this point is not so concerned with making a perfect cadence in A♭ major.

◆ ◆ ◆

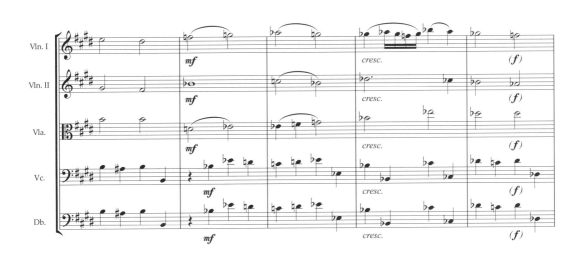

The story of tonality in the symphony from its classical origins through to the end of the nineteenth century is complex and it is important not to oversimplify it. While the classical strategy of cultivating a very strong reliance on the two harmonic pillars of tonic and dominant may have become somewhat old-fashioned after Wagner in the mid-nineteenth century, it by no means died out, and this very clear-cut approach to tonal structure can be seen even in large-scale works in the twentieth century. William Walton's First Symphony, premièred in 1934, provides ample evidence of this. While many late-nineteenth-century composers continued to expand the tonal possibilities of the symphony, it remained a relatively conservative genre, largely because of the need to appeal to large audiences. That said, the gradual loosening of the relationship between tonic and dominant is perceptible even from Haydn's time; after Wagner, tonal innovation and chromaticism were an integral part of symphonic practice.

POINTS FOR FURTHER DISCUSSION

- Compare the expositions of Symphony No. 104 in D 'London' (Haydn) and Symphony No. 1 in G (Bologne). How are they similar? How are they different?
- Discuss tonality in the introduction to Symphony No. 1 in C (Beethoven).
- How did Wagner's ideas of *Leitmotif* and unending melody affect symphonic composition in the late nineteenth century?
- Discuss the relationship between form and tonality in the development of the symphony in the nineteenth century.
- How did eighteenth-century composers balance the requirements of the four-movement symphonic form with expressions of their own individual musical ideas? Refer to at least two of these examples:
    - Symphony No. 1 in G (Bologne)
    - Symphony No. 104 in D, 'London' (Haydn)
    - Symphony No. 1 in C (Beethoven)
    - Symphony No. 4 in A, 'Italian' (Mendelssohn)

Part III: Ideas

8
Absolute music and programme music

Musical meaning is a strange thing when it comes to instrumental music. After all, music is just sound – it doesn't necessarily have any words to clarify what it might be communicating. Discussions about meaning in music become increasingly important as we get further and further into the nineteenth century, and the idea of the 'War of the Romantics' is a crucial lens through which we can understand the ongoing debates, disagreements, and controversies surrounding the symphony in this era. While European orchestral composition in the later part of the eighteenth century is often understood as projecting a unified style, with Vienna and its three big names – Haydn, Mozart, and Beethoven – as its centre of gravity, music in the nineteenth century tells the story of how this style fractured, diversified, and ended up coalescing into two factions who engaged in all sorts of arguments and disagreements. Key issues here include the concept of 'Beethoven's shadow', the idea that Beethoven was a towering figure at the beginning of the nineteenth century and that his influence was felt increasingly strongly in the decades that followed. It didn't matter who you were, you couldn't get away from the influence of Beethoven, and composers had to respond to it somehow because it was simply impossible to ignore. The War of the Romantics was a prolonged series of exchanges between key players within the romantic movement. The distinction between **programme music**, which involves allusions or specific references to extra-musical ideas, was set in opposition to **absolute music**, which describes repertoire that doesn't refer to anything outside itself (not overtly, at least) but is conceived as an abstract structure in sound.

Programme music

Symphonies were often given titles in the classical period, for instance, Haydn's 'Surprise' Symphony, No. 94 in G, whose nickname most obviously references the loud bang near the beginning of the slow movement (although the work does contain other surprises!). It was also common in this era for symphonies to be named after the places where they were first performed (for instance, Haydn's 'London' Symphony, Mozart's 'Prague' Symphony, and so on). This is not programme music, though. Such titles do not give very much away in terms of anything the composer may have been trying to communicate musically, and a fulfilling musical experience would be accessible without knowing the nickname in those cases.

As the symphony progressed into the nineteenth century, especially in the hands of Beethoven, it started to move into more overtly programmatic territory. Beethoven's Third

Symphony, the 'Eroica', alludes to a general idea of heroism that is specifically associated with Napoleon Bonaparte. We know that Beethoven had a troubled impression of the French leader, first dedicating his symphony to Napoleon as someone who freed the French people from the tyranny of monarchy, and then renouncing that dedication. The legend goes that he screwed up the title page after Napoleon declared himself an emperor, later rededicating the work to Prince Lobkowitz. What is clear, however, is that there was some kind of idea originating from outside of the music itself, without which we would only be able to have an incomplete experience of the work. Then we have **Beethoven's 'Pastoral' Symphony, No. 6 in F major**, which goes a step further. In that particular work each of the movements has a descriptive title. So, for example, the first movement is entitled 'Awakening of cheerful feelings on arrival in the countryside'. The slow movement depicts a scene by a babbling brook, and if you listen to the last few minutes of that movement you'll hear specific references to different bird calls: cuckoo, quail, and nightingale played by clarinet, oboe, and flute (**EX. 8.1**). There's a storm-type movement after a peasants' folk dance, before the clearing of the storm and a pastoral finale. These ideas are all borrowed from outside of the musical work, but are depicted in the symphony without the aid of any sounding text, only titles in the score. The Ninth Symphony, by contrast, is much more explicit. After the 'abstract' first three movements, Beethoven uses the text of Schiller's *Ode to Joy* in the finale, sung by a large choir and soloists, clearly taking something from outside of the musical domain and incorporating it into the genre of the symphony.

The generation after Beethoven took the idea of using extra-musical ideas to the next level. Let's consider three key figures: Berlioz, Wagner, and Liszt. First we have the French composer Hector Berlioz (1803–1869) who was responsible for developing the fully fledged programme symphony. His first two symphonies, *Symphonie Fantastique* (1830) and *Harold en Italie* (1834), both in their own ways take a story and try to represent that in sound. *Harold en Italie* takes its cue from Lord Byron's *Childe Harold*, a character represented by obbligato viola, a solo part written for the virtuoso Paganini. This is a very interesting example of how to balance the narrative requirements of a programme with the musical requirements of a symphony. With the programme symphony, two things are going on in tandem. It's no good to compose a four-movement symphonic work that makes sense simply on its own terms. The programme symphony has to make sense in the context of the story that's being progressed, so it's interesting to think how each of the movements does the work of progressing the narrative while also making a musically convincing effect.

EX. 8.1 BEETHOVEN, SYMPHONY NO. 6 IN F, OP. 68, 'PASTORAL', II

CASE STUDY: *SYMPHONIE FANTASTIQUE* (1830) BY HECTOR BERLIOZ

In the case of the *Symphonie Fantastique*, we have a five-movement work which tells the bleak story of a young artist who poisons himself with opiates in response to his despair over unrequited love, ending with him witnessing his own execution. The way Berlioz links the movements to make sense of the narrative while remaining musically convincing is via an **idée fixe** (**EX. 8.2**) – a preoccupation that dominates the mind, or in this case, a recurring motif that underpins the whole work – which represents 'The Beloved'.

This *idée fixe* is changed in each movement to reflect the particular episode in the Artist's obsession with The Beloved. Berlioz's programmatic writing is particularly explicit in the fourth and fifth movements of the work. Of the fourth movement, the 'March to the Scaffold', Berlioz wrote in his programme note:

> The artist, now knowing beyond all doubt that his love is not returned, poisons himself with opium. The dose of the narcotic, too weak to take his life, plunges him into a sleep accompanied by the most horrible visions. He dreams that he has killed the woman that he loved, and that he is condemned to death, brought to the scaffold, and witnesses *his own execution*. The procession is accompanied by a march that is sometimes fierce and sombre, sometimes stately and brilliant: loud crashes are followed abruptly by the dull thud of heavy footfalls. At the end of the march, the first four bars of the *idée fixe* recur like a last thought of love interrupted by the fatal stroke.[1]

Berlioz achieves these key narrative points through his use of both the orchestra and his use of the *idée fixe*. At the very opening of the movement, the timpani depict the Artist being led to his execution, accompanied by cellos and double basses divided into four low parts (**EX. 8.3**). At the end of the movement, after we have heard depictions of the grotesque marches of a public execution, the *idée fixe* briefly sounds on clarinet, reminding us that his obsession with The Beloved is occupying his mind even in the last moments of his life. This is cut short by a massive chord representing the guillotine's blade falling, and we then hear the Artist's head bouncing down the steps (heard in the *pizzicato* strings) as the drums roll and the crowds cheer (**EX. 8.4**).

---

1   Hector Berlioz, *Symphonie Fantastique*, Ernst Eulenberg Ltd, 1977, xvii.

EX. 8.3 BERLIOZ, *SYMPHONIE FANTASTIQUE*, IV, BARS 1–5, MARCH TO THE SCAFFOLD

EX. 8.4 BERLIOZ, *SYMPHONIE FANTASTIQUE*, IV, BARS 162–178

Crowds cheer

The fifth movement presents a vision of a Satanic 'Dream of a Witches' Sabbath'. Of this, Berlioz wrote:

> He is surrounded by a hideous throng of demons and sorcerers, gathered to cele-
> brate Sabbath night . . . At last the *melody* arrives. Till then it had appeared only in a
> graceful guise, but now it has become a vulgar tavern tune, trivial and base; the beloved
> object has come to the Sabbath to take part in her victim's funeral. She is nothing but
> a courtesan, fit to figure in the orgy. The ceremony begins; the bells toll, the whole
> hellish cohort prostrates itself; a chorus chants the plainsong sequence of the dead,
> two other choruses repeat it in a burlesque parody. Finally, the Sabbath round-dance
> whirls. At its violent climax it mingles with the Dies irae, and the vision ends.[2]

Violins and violas, divided into eight parts, open the movement playing a high *tremolo* to create an otherworldly soundscape (**EX. 8.5A**). This nightmarish mood is reinforced by idiomatic
techniques such as **portamenti** in the woodwind (**EX. 8.5B**).

EX. 8.5A BERLIOZ, *SYMPHONIE FANTASTIQUE*, V, BARS 1–2, STRINGS

2   Hector Berlioz, *Symphonie Fantastique*, Ernst Eulenberg Ltd, 1977, xvii.

EX. 8.5B BERLIOZ, *SYMPHONIE FANTASTIQUE*, V, BARS 17–19

EX. 8.6 BERLIOZ, *SYMPHONIE FANTASTIQUE*, V, BARS 40–65

Later in the movement, the *idée fixe* is heard on the high E♭ clarinet, which until then had not been used in the orchestra. This paints a shrill, distorted version of the Beloved (**EX. 8.6**). Berlioz then brings in pre-existing musical material with the *Dies Irae* – a Gregorian chant quoted by many composers to represent death and wrath. Eventually, the witches' round dance motif becomes a frenetic, wild tune played by the strings that then battles with loud statements of the *Dies Irae* (wind and brass) (**EX. 8.7**). This is followed by the most extensive symphonic use of **col legno** until that point. Here Berlioz uses the technique to imitate the sound of skeletons dancing to another variation of the witches' round dance, this time heavily distorted with trills (bars 445–460).

EX. 8.7 BERLIOZ, *SYMPHONIE FANTASTIQUE*, V, BARS 414–421

Wagner was responsible for the **Gesamtkunstwerk**. This involved taking different art forms – poetry, scenery, costume, architecture, and music – and combining them into a colossal 'complete art work'. This is expressed in his music dramas – huge operatic works dealing with epic subject matter and lasting hours in performance. Before Wagner, the normal way of writing opera would have been for a composer and a librettist to collaborate; the writing of the text and the music would have been seen as separate tasks. Wagner, however, took complete control of the creative process: he wrote the texts, he wrote the music, and he even designed the opera house at Bayreuth. Although Wagner only completed one symphony (which is rarely performed nowadays), his influence on instrumental composition in the second half of the nineteenth century was keenly felt. Along with his progressive chromatic harmony and complex contrapuntal style, Wagner is also credited with developing the technique of 'unending melody' (see chapter 4). We are used in the classical period to a neat, closed musical framework and syntax in which cadential closure serves to define themes and keys. Wagner, by contrast, was interested in prolonging musical tension through continuous drama. The idea of unending melody, then, is that we very rarely reach a point of finality – a cadence – and perhaps not until the very end of the opera which could last more than four hours.

Wagner's approach to melody and closure had a lasting influence on important late nineteenth-century Austro-German symphonists, especially Bruckner, but also outside of the German-speaking area of central Europe. By revisiting the secondary theme from the first movement of **Tchaikovsky's Sixth Symphony** which we first encountered in chapter 4 (**EX. 8.8**) we can see that it never produces a perfect cadence with the tonic in the melody (the strongest kind of cadence), but rather it seems to linger, only to be interrupted by the loud announcement of the movement's developmental section.

Lastly, we have Franz Liszt, who is credited with developing the new genre of the symphonic poem, sometimes called a **tone poem** (from the German, *Tondichtung*). This is usually a one-movement work for orchestra, although it can contain more than one movement. It again takes its basis from some kind of extra-musical text or idea and tells the story through music. With these sorts of pieces, familiarity with the background of the text is necessary before a full understanding of the music is possible. The extra-musical stimulus often comes from a literary source – *Hamlet* (1858) draws on Shakespeare's play, and *Tasso: lamento e trionfo* (1854–1856) draws on texts by Goethe and Byron – but Liszt's regular practice was to provide his own written preface to each work, detailing the narrative events that the music depicts. Of course, you can listen to the piece of music and it might make perfect sense on its own; but without knowledge of the paratext, much of the communicative intent behind the composition will be lost.

EX. 8.8 TCHAIKOVSKY, SYMPHONY NO. 6 IN B MINOR, 'PATHÉTIQUE', I, BARS 153–166

Absolute music

The other side of the debate involved a number of composers and thinkers, the most import-ant of whom was Eduard Hanslick (1825–1904) who wrote a very important study entitled 'On the Beautiful in Music' (*Vom Musikalisch-Schönen*). This was first published in 1854 and proved to be a decisive moment in musical aesthetics. Hanslick was not a composer, or at least not a professional one, but he was an important nineteenth-century aesthetician and his controver-sial ideas continue to be debated today. Hanslick was critical of Wagner and Liszt, arguing that music can arouse feelings and emotions, but it cannot represent them; he argued that feelings and emotions are part of the listening experience but that they are not in any respect 'in the music'. For Hanslick, music at its most powerful was an abstract and absolute art, not to be mixed with extra-musical ideas. He argued that truly great music is self-standing and transcen-dent – it has the ability to overcome the normal thresholds of human experience, to achieve something that is not possible in the other arts. The opposite of this approach, in Hanslick's view, was the type of extra-musical programme, used by Liszt and others, which somehow acted as a crutch that weaker composers used to prop up their music. Such music was some-how weak or deficient, and these composers were using the idea of a programme as a way of 'explaining' their music; if they were truly great composers, Hanslick argued, their music would not require any explanation but would stand on its own.

It would be simplistic to understand the opposing concepts of 'absolute' and 'programme' music as encapsulating all nineteenth-century symphonic practice. There is always a tension between the two. On one side we have so-called absolute music – we say 'so-called' because it is difficult to imagine a composition that really is completely self-sufficient, not reliant on anything outside of itself. Whenever we listen to a piece of music we always bring with us all of our previous experiences of playing and listening, and composers are also working within a set of conventions, a bit like a language, which existed before they embarked on the creative process. We can, however, acknowledge that the *pursuit* of absolute music was a reality in the nineteenth century, expressed in the large number of symphonies which bear a number and a key but no text or title (e.g., Brahms's Symphony No. 1 in C minor), giving nothing away and leaving considerations of any 'meaning' or communicative content open to diverse interpre-tations. There is, however, a theme in the finale of Brahms's First Symphony which is a refer-ence to the *Ode to Joy* from Beethoven's Ninth Symphony (the similarity is shown in EX. 8.9A and EX. 8.9B). Once this has been registered and acknowledged, the music stops being purely abstract and begins to reference things outside of itself. The 'purely abstract symphony' is a useful idea for understanding certain approaches to composition, but finding true examples of it is difficult. There is always something – a theme, an idea, a timbre, a mood – that connects it by association with something else.

EX. 8.9A THEME IN BRAHMS, SYMPHONY NO. 1, IV, BARS 61–77

EX. 8.9B *ODE TO JOY* IN BEETHOVEN, SYMPHONY NO. 9, IV, BARS 92–107

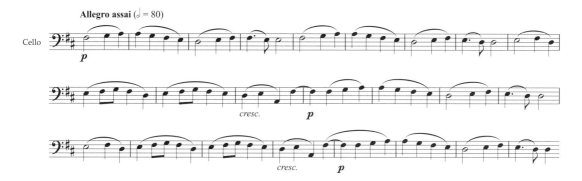

The above example of Brahms referencing Beethoven can be understood as a dialogue with a tradition, in this case the tradition of composing a 'choral-style' finale (even though it doesn't literally use a choir). This became a tradition after Beethoven, which Brahms references. In other words, the music enters into a dialogue with that tradition on the basis that it is installed in that mode of listening, with the expectation that audiences might bring that tradition with them to a performance of that work. Other dialogues with tradition exist and are strongly expressed in the repertoire. The choice of key that a composer makes, for example, can automatically invoke a tradition (more on this below!).

Similarly, we sometimes find composers using popular or folk melodies or imitations of those vernacular styles in their music to serve political or nationalistic purposes. These can act as a signpost highlighting where the work came from. We do sometimes find this in the Austro-Germanic symphonic output, but it's much more common outside of Germany. Many composers were trying to stake a claim to the genre for their own country, and the symphonies of Dvořák provide some characteristic 'Slavonic' themes more usually associated with dance music (the Scherzo of his Seventh Symphony in D minor, for example, is generically barely distinguishable from his many Slavonic Dances).

Unlike the full programme symphony, which would have been quite explicit in its narrative aims, it was also possible to imply a programme without stating it. Sometimes some loosely organised programmatic content can even be projected onto a work in the course of its reception. Tchaikovsky's last symphony (No. 6 in B minor) is a good example. This was his final composition before dying in mysterious circumstances, and autobiographical interpretations have proliferated ever since. The symphony's B minor tonality is already a very specific choice of key, rare in eighteenth- and nineteenth-century orchestral music. Schubert's Eighth Symphony and

Borodin's Second are the other two important symphonic exceptions, and B minor was closely associated with the death of Christ after J. S. Bach's monumental mass in that key. The music at the end of Tchaikovsky's finale seems to die away into nothing, and it's also arguably the first symphony to have a slow finale (although Mahler's Third was completed around the same time, there is no evidence that the two composers corresponded). The work ends in a low, deathly B minor, which is a very unusual thing to do: symphonies normally end triumphantly, but this is no crowd pleaser. Tchaikovsky died less than two weeks after the première of that work after apparently deliberately drinking tap water (which in nineteenth-century St Petersburg would have led to cholera and certain death).

The War of the Romantics

The symphonic tradition in the late eighteenth and the early nineteenth centuries is usually considered to be an Austro-German one with Beethoven as the genre's centre of gravity. This is arguably a fiction, given the number of composers who were working in Vienna around the same time as Beethoven (which included Wanhal, Dittersdorf, and Hofmann, who each enjoyed degrees of success). Beethoven was just one figure, which history constructs as a singular genius. However, the centrality of Beethoven as he was perceived during the course of the nineteenth century was not fictional: this was absolutely real and would shape the direction of symphonic music from the first decades of that century through to the present day.

The sense of a split in the symphonic tradition is palpable from the 1830s onward. A certain group of composers, notably Schubert, Mendelssohn, Schumann, and somewhat later in the century, Brahms, strove to continue what was in its essence a tradition inherited in the first place from Haydn and Mozart, and amplified through the 'absolute' symphonic music of Beethoven. These composers were interested in the traditional genres of the symphony, quartet, and sonata. They continued to compose works comprising four movements with no specific programme. While this may seem a conservative strategy, there are many examples of progressiveness in each composer's output. This tradition's association with Leipzig is crucial. After Mendelssohn had established the Conservatory of Music there in 1843, Leipzig became an important seat of learning for that particular tradition of symphonic and sonata composition. It became *de rigueur* for aspiring musicians to gain qualifications from the conservatory, and it boasts many famous graduates, including the English composers Arthur Sullivan and Ethel Smyth, the Norwegian Edvard Grieg, and the Czech Leoš Janáček.

On the other side, we have a group of composers that coalesced into an association called the New German School. The progressive programmaticists Liszt and Wagner were two of the important figures in this group. We can compare and contrast these two different schools, pointing out their differences and the arguments and controversies that simmered during the middle part of the nineteenth century. Interestingly, though, both sides viewed Beethoven as the root of their tradition. The Leipzig school saw Beethoven's symphonies as the proper place to draw influence in terms of writing abstract music in the classical tradition. For the New German School, the fact that Beethoven by the end of his Ninth Symphony seemed to have decided that he could go no further with instruments alone, and that music had to break into song at the pivotal moment in the finale, was the starting point for them. Interestingly, Wagner considered his own music dramas to be the natural progression from the symphony, which by mid-century was perceived to have run its course. James Hepokoski summarises this situation neatly:

> It may seem one of the ironies of nineteenth-century music that the perception of a crisis within Austro-German sonata construction set in at almost precisely the same time as the emergence of the academic recognition and honouring of this tradition, most notably in A.B. Marx's *Die Lehre von der musikalischen Komposition, praktisch-theoretisch* (1838).[2]

Hepokoski is arguing that it was really after this tradition of symphonic composition was already 'dead' that it started to be theorised. In 1838, A.B. Marx was one of the earliest theorists to discuss musical form in that particular way, but of course by that time Beethoven and Schubert had been dead for ten years, and Haydn and Mozart were long gone. Mendelssohn and Schumann were still composing, but by the time that this kind of **Formenlehre** tradition had really taken hold around 1850, Mendelssohn was dead, and Schumann, although he wasn't at the end of his life, had been suffering from severe mental illness. He spent the last two years of his life in a sanatorium in Bonn, where he died in 1856.[3]

So we have a gap in the middle of the nineteenth century when the Beethovenian tradition of 'absolute' music was on the wane. The New German School emerged as the dominant force in European orchestral composition, represented in the new genres of the Wagnerian music drama, the programme symphony, and the tone poem. It is commonplace to think of the nineteenth century as the 'great age of the symphony'; in fact, the genre was in chaos during the 1850s and 1860s, with two competing visions of its future, both claiming Beethoven as their model. These tensions persisted and shaped the development of the genre for the rest of the century. Rather than dividing practice into two neatly organised factions, however, it is often more productive to locate different composers and their compositions at various points along a spectrum between programme music and absolute music. Next, let's look at two of the most important Beethovenian traditions which developed through the nineteenth century.

---

2   James Hepokoski, 'Beethoven reception: the symphonic tradition', *The Cambridge History of Nineteenth Century Music*, Ed. Jim Samson (Cambridge: CUP, 2001), 425.

3   The German term *Formenlehre* literally means the 'teaching of form' and was an important theoretical tradition in the nineteenth century, now enjoying a renaissance in the twenty-first century (the so-called 'New Formenlehre').

The heroic tradition

Of the many 'Beethoven traditions' that proliferated in the nineteenth century, the heroic tradition is probably the most important. Beethoven's Third Symphony, the 'Eroica', is the *locus classicus* for this, and from this time (1804), heroism in instrumental music would be associated with the key of E♭ major. The 'heroic' symphony may have been nascent in the classical period – Mozart did write an E♭, heroic-type symphony, No. 39, which also resembles Beethoven's work in a few salient details. Along with the three flats in the key signature, both works' first-movement sonata forms are set in triple metre. The rule of three becomes stronger from Beethoven onward: Beethoven's 'Eroica' is his Third Symphony and it uses three horns instead of the usual two. There are many other examples. Schumann's Third Symphony is in E♭ major (1850) and begins with a first movement in triple metre. Interestingly, E♭ in this work is also associated with the River Rhine (hence, the title of the work, 'Rhenish'). This key is also the starting point of Wagner's opera *Das Rheingold* (the first instalment of his epic four-part 'Ring Cycle'), which begins with an extended *Klang* consisting of increasingly intense motion in the eight horn parts revolving around an E♭ major triad. So E♭ is now associated with heroism as well as the Rhine. Both are also associated with the use of French horns. Something as abstract as a key signature can bring a context in which we can interpret the apparently 'absolute' music.

Brahms also composed a symphony in this heroic tradition: his Third in F major (1883). Although Brahms chose a different key for this one, the mood and tempo summon the Beethovenian heroic inheritance. The $\frac{6}{4}$ metre of the opening movement (a favoured time signature for Brahms) generates a more expansive effect than the $\frac{3}{4}$ of Beethoven's and Schumann's contributions, but nevertheless it shares the heroic mood.

It is also possible to find symphonies in the heroic tradition outside of Austria and Germany. The Russian composer Alexander Borodin (mainly famous for his work in the field of chemistry!) composed a First Symphony in E♭ major (completed in 1867) with a fast-tempo triple-metre first movement, making prominent use of that most heroic of instruments: the French horn.

The pastoral tradition

Depictions of landscape were common in all sorts of music in the eighteenth century and before. It had been particularly popular in opera, in which composers constructed a kind of Arcadian, pastoral, idyllic world where humanity was in balance with nature (Handel's *Acis and Galatea* is a representative example of this, and there are many others from the Italian, French, and English repertoire of the seventeenth and eighteenth centuries). From around the 1750s, the pastoral topic was already a well-established context for symphonic music that composers could draw on. Pastoral or 'landscape' music could appear at more or less any point in a symphony, though many composers were keen to exploit its more reflective qualities in gently lilting, $\frac{6}{8}$ Andante movements (such as the one found in **Mozart's 'Prague' Symphony, No. 38 in D**, EX. 8.10). Rustic or vernacular elements were also common, and included drones and folk-like melodies. In **Haydn's Symphony No. 88 in G** (EX. 8.11) this occurs in the more relaxed Trio section of the Minuet movement where the drone can be heard in the bassoons and violas, underpinning a pastoral melody in the oboe and violins.

EX. 8.10 MOZART, SYMPHONY NO. 38 IN D, 'PRAGUE', II, BARS 1–7

By around 1800 the prospect of a whole symphony being suffused with the pastoral topic became a distinct possibility, and after Beethoven's 'Pastoral' Symphony (1808), if it had ever been in any doubt, F major would become a permanent home of the pastoral mood. In Beethoven's case, each of his symphony's five movements depicts a different aspect of nature. The fourth movement depicts its terrifying alter-ego as a stormy, destructive force with the use of the *tempesta* topic and the negatively charged alternative key of F minor. This was a kind of local pastoralism that is sometimes associated with **Biedermeier Vienna**, at a time when the visual arts and music were catering to a middle-class audience and referring to countryside that could be experienced a short walk from the city.[4]

Mendelssohn's landscape music is a more exotic type of pastoralism – not the local pastoralism of Beethoven, but the landscape of somewhere less familiar, for instance, Italy or Scotland. His Symphony No. 4, the 'Italian', depicts elements of Italian life and landscape. Examples of this include a particular Italian dance in the last movement (the *saltarello*) and the slow movement which depicts a religious procession that the composer witnessed during a trip to Naples. Even in the more 'abstract' first movement's sonata form we can draw attention to features such as the brightness and crispness of the orchestration (owing, partly, to the use of the high horns in A, the highest horns available at that time), which Mendelssohn described as 'blue sky in A major'. We might contrast this with the dark, murky opening of his 'Scottish' Symphony in A minor, whose first bars blend violas and woodwind, low in their register, creating a much more foggy and indistinct landscape – one in which the outline of distant mountains is more difficult to make out. The work also borrows stylistically from Scottish folk music, especially in the lively second movement (taking the place of the normative Scherzo), though it seems that this particular clarinet tune is entirely of Mendelssohn's making and not a direct quotation of any actual folk melody.

Dvořák's Fifth Symphony in F (1875) is another pastoral work. Though it does not bear the title 'Pastoral', you only need to listen to the first few bars to hear the musical evocation of nature and a sense of pastoralism through devices such as drones and through particular choices of instrumentation (the two soli clarinets right at the beginning immediately set the mood). Another F major symphony, the Third of Joachim Raff (1822–1882; the work was completed in 1869) entitled *Im Walde* ('In the Woods') serves further to confirm that key as the locus of nineteenth-century symphonic pastoralism. We can also add minor-mode contributions to this tradition, including Borodin's Second Symphony in A minor (1887, completed by Glazunov). The work opens with unaccompanied oboe which, from at least as far back as Handel, was inextricably linked to pastoralism and the romanticised image of the lonely shepherd with his pipe.

While such pastoralism in the nineteenth-century symphony remained double-edged after the storm in Beethoven's Sixth (precipitating stormy passages in subsequent pastoral works, including Mendelssohn's Third, Dvořák's Fifth, and many others), the overall mood of the pastoral topic during these decades remained a positively affirmative one. The harmonious balance of nature and humanity usually framed (and therefore overcame) the internal depictions of a stormy or otherwise cruelly indifferent nature. This paradigm came under scrutiny later in the century, however, as Gustav Mahler began to give it a darker tone, perhaps drawing attention not to the

4   The term *Biedermeier* describes the prevailing middle-class culture in Vienna and other areas of central Europe from the end of the Napoleonic wars until the mid-century revolutions, from 1815 to 1848.

harmony between humanity and nature, but their disjunction as the increasingly industrialised European economies began to draw people away from the countryside and into the cities.

Evocations of the calm serenity of the landscape and of the romanticised rustic purity of folk music can still be found in Mahler's symphonies. Examples abound in his First Symphony, first performed in 1889, but they are often tainted or jeopardised in the way they are presented. For example, the primary theme of the symphony's first movement – a borrowing from an earlier composition, 'Ging heut' Morgen über's Feld', the second song from Mahler's *Lieder eines fahrenden Gesellen* – is presented as a carefree pastoral topic with the usual drones and folk-like melodic shapes. But it is preceded by an introduction and followed by the start of the development section that shares material of a much darker quality, thereby reversing the normal pattern of idyll–storm–idyll.

While much of Mahler's pastoral music seems to be jeopardised or conditional in nature, it is just as often modally tainted, being presented in a minor key. We find a memorable example of this in the slow movement (here in third place and not the traditional second) of the same symphony. Aside from the grim opening music, which presents the popular children's song *Frère Jacques* in a deeply unsettling D minor, the middle of the movement seems almost to teleport us out of the urban setting of the concert hall and to materialise in the rural context of a klezmer band. While this could be a reference to the composer's Jewish cultural background, it also performs the unusual manoeuvre of aligning the pastoral topic (outside of the classical *tempesta* found in Beethoven or Mendelssohn) with the minor mode, thereby raising a question about its consoling or restorative qualities. This tradition of so-called 'dark pastoralism' would gain momentum into the twentieth century, and can be found in many Nordic and British symphonies, with important examples including Jean Sibelius's Second Symphony in D (another pastoral key!), Carl Nielsen's Third and Sixth Symphonies, and especially Ralph Vaughan Williams's 'Pastoral' Symphony. This was composed shortly after the First World War, a context in which Vaughan Williams's pastoralism referred not to idyllic countryside, but rather the hollowed-out fields of Flanders.

◆   ◆   ◆

One of the stories of the nineteenth-century symphony was the way in which Beethovenian forms acted as a starting point – a sort of blank canvas – onto which later composers could stake a claim and project their own ideas. Beethoven's shadow was at once an oppressive condition that composers felt a need to respond to and react against, but also an important creative stimulus for both composers of the classicising tendency who were interested in the tradition of absolute music (most notably Mendelssohn and Brahms), and composers of the New German School who were responsible for some important generic upheavals that would put a question to the symphony as a genre. From the middle of the nineteenth century, it became a statement, a conscious choice, to compose a symphony with no title and no programme, thereby aligning oneself with the absolute-music tradition. The set of generic options – which now included the programme symphony and the tone poem – would be pivotal for a new generation of symphonists from outside of the Austro-German tradition, and it is to these composers that we direct our attention in the next chapter.

9

The symphony outside Germany and Austria

To what extent is the symphony an Austro-German genre? It may appear at first glance that the German-speaking area of Central and Northern Europe completely dominated symphonic composition in the eighteenth and nineteenth centuries, with important centres such as Mannheim, Leipzig, Berlin, and especially Vienna having a pivotal role in the development of this repertoire. While there may be some truth to this, it doesn't give a complete picture of the compositional and concert activity that was happening at the time. This situation is largely because of the concept of the canon – an established repertoire of musical works – that began to regulate musical practice from around 1800.[1] The canon has always privileged Austrian and German composers working in 'public' genres such as the symphony and this has led to a very short and exclusive list of men whose music has been in permanent circulation over the years. The symphonists in this group can easily be listed: Haydn, Mozart, Beethoven, Schubert, Mendelssohn, Schumann, Brahms, Bruckner, and Mahler. There are many problems with restricting ourselves to such a group of composers, and this has led to sustained criticism about limiting the study of music simply to 'dead white German men' – hardly a group representative of the much broader category: 'music'.

While these criticisms will continue to be debated, in this chapter we'll open up the discussion to engage one of the important limiting factors of the canon: geography. It stands to reason that we should give plenty of focus to the composers listed above, but Austria and Germany were not the only places where symphonies were being composed and performed. The fact that the symphony first emerged from the genres of the concerto and the overture – both Italian in origin – is reason enough to look further afield. It is also important to note that even within the elite group listed above there is already a large degree of geographical diversity. Germany did not exist as a country until the majority of the German states unified in 1871, and each state would have continued with its own local traditions. Austria existed as an empire during this time, and although Vienna was undoubtedly an important cultural centre, musical traditions within the Austro-Hungarian Empire were not uniform. A case in point is Gustav Mahler (more on him in the next chapter), who worked for most of his career in Vienna but originally came from Jihlava, a town which was then in Moravia, part of Austro-Hungary, but which nowadays is in the Czech Republic. Even Beethoven stretches the imagination of what it means to be a German composer. His birthplace, the city of Bonn, which sits on the banks of

---

1   Lydia Goehr, *The Imaginary Museum of Musical Works* (revised edition, Oxford: Oxford University Press, 2007).

THE SYMPHONY OUTSIDE GERMANY AND AUSTRIA 157

the River Rhein on the western fringe of Germany, would have been considered a border town with the Netherlands during the eighteenth century, and this Low Countries influence can be detected in his name: he was apparently very proud of the Dutch-sounding 'van', as opposed to the Germanic 'von'.

In the period 1750–1900 the symphony was overwhelmingly a Northern European phenomenon. The geographical area in which symphonic composition was an important part of musical life shifted, however, and grew during the nineteenth century. The idea of national styles, which had been pivotal in the early eighteenth century (think of J. S. Bach's 'French' and 'English' Suites and his 'Italian' Concerto) began to coalesce into a unified classical musical language as fashions changed, and they changed quickly within the galant style of the mid-eighteenth century. The nineteenth century, by contrast, saw the emergence of dominant national genres. In Germany, the symphony; in France, ballet; in Italy, opera; and in Britain, the oratorio, largely thanks to Handel's countless contributions to be sung in English, later sustained by Mendelssohn and a string of minor English composers. The symphony, however, became an important genre in many areas of Northern and Eastern Europe, especially with the increasing importance of musical nationalism, for which it proved an important vessel.

Early non-German symphonists included the Bohemian innovator Johann Stamitz (Jan Stamic in Czech) who we have heard plenty about in previous chapters. The Italian Giovanni Sammartini, although his birthplace of Milan was then in Habsburg-ruled Lombardy, was an important Southern European innovator who is credited with turning the light-hearted operatic overture into the more serious instrumental genre that we now recognise as the symphony. The much younger Italian (and later Spanish) composer Luigi Boccherini (1743–1805) was a prolific symphonist who completed at least 30 works bearing the title, and many more which seem to bridge the gap between the symphony and the concerto. Really to tie these composers to a particular nationality is to miss the point, however. These were cosmopolitan craftsmen who were prepared to travel across political, geographical, and linguistic borders in search of a position where they could hone their craft. For many of these composers, finding such a position meant heading north, and 'heading north' was associated with one place in particular.

United Kingdom

The German critic Oscar Schmitz pointedly claimed in 1914 that England was 'Das Land ohne Musik' (the country without music), on the basis that it had been unable (or unwilling) to sustain its own musical tradition.[2] While this is a manifestly unfair claim, it is also true that we have to look a long way back to find a British composer who occupies as secure a place in the canon as Haydn or Mendelssohn. **Henry Purcell** (1659–1695) was really the last native Englishman to enjoy any level of enduring fame or success until Edward Elgar exploded onto the scene more than 200 years later. However, it also has to be said that in London the UK boasted one of the most important and lively concert-giving cities in Europe in the late eighteenth and nineteenth centuries, and along with a handful of lesser-known native composers, London was an attractive destination for continental musicians.

---

2   Oscar A.H. Schmitz, *Das Land ohne Musik: Englische Gesellschaftsproblemer*, Munich, 1914.

One of these lesser-known Englishmen was **William Boyce** (1711–1779), whose eight symphonies were published in London as his Op. 2 in 1760. These short works would have been conceived independently of the innovations that were going on in Mannheim and other European musical centres, and therefore come across as being more heavily indebted to the earlier contrapuntal idiom that had been inherited from Handel. Each of these symphonies was conceived as an overture to a more substantial vocal work and they were collected over a period of two decades before being published together as a set. Boyce's symphonies, all of which were scored for oboes, horns, strings, and continuo, really demonstrate the functional nature of the genre in the mid-eighteenth century – a genre that served an external purpose and was not intended for its own sake.

Of the many continental visitors to London in the eighteenth century, **Johann Christian Bach** (1735–1782) was one of the most prolific and successful. J. C. Bach was the eleventh son and the eighteenth child of the (then obscure) baroque composer, J. S. Bach. Although Johann Christian followed in his father's footsteps by pursuing a career as a composer, it was there that the similarities stopped. J. C. Bach enjoyed much more success and fame in his own lifetime than his father ever did, composing in a style that sharply contrasted with the densely polyphonic music of the earlier generation. Johann Christian moved to London in 1762, where he composed well over 30 symphonies, many in his role as Master of Music to Queen Charlotte. Some of these have been lost – this was before the era of published scores, so this music would have existed only in the orchestral parts and in the memories of listeners – but those that have survived are a demonstration that eighteenth-century symphonic composition in London was at least as exciting and inventive as anything that was going on in Mannheim or Vienna at the time.

While the fashion and desire to hear exotic music of continental composers in London was at a high point at the turn of the nineteenth century, in later decades there was an increasing feeling that the UK needed to project its own musical voice and not rely so much on repertoire imported from the continent. The perception of a gap in the repertoire that was in need of attention began to gather pace from around the middle of the nineteenth century and eventually coalesced into what historians now call the 'English musical renaissance'. Not to be confused with 'the renaissance' (the fifteenth-century rediscovery of ancient art, literature, and science that started in Florence), the English musical renaissance was a slow and fairly disorderly process of building up a native classical repertoire, supported by institutions such as conservatoires where British musicians could be trained and educated, and concert halls where this music could be performed. **William Sterndale Bennett** (1816–1875) was a key figure in this movement, and though his two symphonies are rarely performed nowadays, he was an important precursor to subsequent generations of English composers. **Hubert Parry** (1848–1918), whose choral music is these days associated with nationalistic pageantry, composed five symphonies that are comparable in length, scope, and orchestration with Brahms's.

Symphonic composition in the second half of the nineteenth century was understood as a rite of passage: many composers would write in the genre as a demonstration of their command of the musical materials before later moving on to concentrate on other things. The London-born Samuel Coleridge-Taylor's (1875–1912) Symphony in A minor (1896) represents a youthful contribution to the genre. **Arthur Sullivan** (1842–1900) is another clear example of this trend, having composed his Symphony in E (nicknamed the 'Irish' Symphony after his death) in 1866 and then abandoning the genre in order to build a career as an opera composer. At the time he composed his Symphony in A minor, Coleridge-Taylor was only in his early twenties. He went on to achieve success in England and especially in America after successful visits across the Atlantic. His symphony is, however, a highly impressive work that is deserving of more regular performance. The golden age of the British symphony, which began with the first performance of Elgar's First Symphony in 1907 and reached a point of maximum intensity in the 1930s with new large-scale works being produced apace by Ralph Vaughan Williams, William Walton, Edmund Rubbra, and many others, is beyond the scope of this book.

France and the Low Countries

Although France was not an obvious centre for symphonic activity during the eighteenth century, there are some flashes of brilliance that come to the surface from time to time. We have already heard how the Chevalier de Saint-Georges not only composed two of his own symphonies but also commissioned and conducted the first performances of Haydn's 'Paris' Symphonies. We have also heard about Mozart's early tour to Paris, where he responded (perhaps grudgingly) to French tastes. In a similar way to Britain, the initial importation of symphonic composition from Austria and Germany would eventually spark a self-standing French symphonic tradition.

Given the relative lack of symphonic output in Paris, **Louise Farrenc** (1804–1875) is an unusual voice in nineteenth-century French musical culture. She studied at the Paris Conservatoire before embarking on a career as a concert pianist and later becoming the first female professor of piano at the Paris Conservatoire. In that role she successfully fought for equal pay with her male counterparts. Commentators noted the similarity in her compositional style to that of Robert Schumann – a comparison that endured throughout Farrenc's career – and Schumann was a great admirer of Farrenc's work. Her Third Symphony in G minor stands out as a contribution which runs counter to the prevailing 'darkness-to-light' narrative of the nineteenth century: the work ends resolutely (and perhaps defiantly) in the tonic minor. This gesture puts a question to the old-fashioned notion that music composed by women features 'feminine' characteristics (whatever those might be). To reuse the culinary metaphor we offered in Chapter 2, a female composer is no more likely to write feminine music than a female chef is likely to cook feminine food.

The French composer of English descent **George Onslow** (1784–1853) seems something of an anomaly. Counter to the practice of importing Austrian or German composers who would change their style to suit French tastes, Onslow's four symphonies seem quite closely to follow Austro-German precedents, and as a result he had greater success in Germany and England than he enjoyed in France.

Onslow was elected as Honorary Fellow of the Philharmonic Society of London in 1831, following on from Mendelssohn, and he composed his Second Symphony in D minor for the Society. His style of composition is not dissimilar to Mendelssohn's with its clarity of formal organisation and scoring. It is therefore all the more surprising that Berlioz's colossal *Symphonie Fantastique* had already sent shockwaves through Europe a year earlier. This is a symptom of a generational divide, but also a matter of compositional approach. Onslow's symphony is squarely conceived in the Viennese classical tradition. Berlioz's symphony by contrast is a statement of intent: 'this tradition is dead – we need a new approach!' Berlioz's programme symphonies, the *Symphonie Fantastique* and *Harold en Italie*, would become key texts in the War of the Romantics that would ensue in subsequent decades and would not be resolved for at least another 50 years.

The 17-year-old **Georges Bizet**'s (1838–1875) Symphony in C major (1855) is of interest not only because of the age of the composer but also because of its remarkable success as a piece of absolute music during a time when programmatic composition was in full swing. Some have compared the work with the Symphony in D by his teacher at the Paris Conservatoire, **Charles Gounod** (1818–1893). The two works share notable similarities in structure and content, including some fairly indisputable melodic correspondence, but it seems clear that symphonic composition was something of an academic demonstration of technique rather than an aim in itself for these composers.

The really serious shift in direction came later in the century with **César Franck** (1822–1890, born in Liège which was then in the Netherlands but is currently in Belgium), whose Symphony in D minor (1887–88) opens with a quotation from Liszt's tone poem *Les Préludes*. His music incorporates the progressive harmonic language that Liszt and Wagner had been developing, but he brings this language into an idiom aligned with absolute music. This work is of a different order from previous mid-century contributions by Bizet and Gounod, and its harmonic complexity and cyclic thematic design earn its place in the repertory alongside the most densely worked symphonies of Brahms and Bruckner.

Camille Saint-Saëns (1835–1921) was by far the most important French symphonist after Berlioz, and is sometimes credited with synthesising French melodic and harmonic idioms with a German approach to musical form. After his student symphony in A major, he composed three numbered symphonies. Of these, the most popular and frequently performed is the Third in C minor. Commonly known as Saint-Saëns's 'Organ' Symphony, it has many progressive features, including the incorporation of the organ into the symphonic texture, the joining together of movements one and two (the first movement sonata form dissolving into the reflective D♭ major slow movement) and the joining of movements three and four (the Scherzo 'starting again' in C minor and setting up the triumphal C major finale). Saint-Saëns' use of a chorale melody as the primary thematic idea for this finale aligns the work with other instrumental 'choral' finales, especially that of Brahms's First Symphony. Along with innovative formal decisions, especially in the last movement, Saint-Saëns' use of the piano (very rarely a symphonic instrument) within the orchestral texture – adding an extra player for the crucial accompanying role of the chorale tune for a 'four-hands' texture to support the strings – is inspired.

Russia

Like the UK, Russia had to wait until the twentieth century before it could finally boast its own fully fledged symphonic tradition. We avoid the term 'golden age' here because much of **Dmitri Shostakovich**'s (1906–1975) and **Sergei Prokofiev**'s (1891–1953) orchestral music was penned under Stalin when Russia was part of the Soviet Union, and especially during the 'Great

Terror' of 1936–1938, during which the Soviet authorities repressed the population, leading to the deaths of an estimated one million of its citizens. While this twentieth-century repertoire is often understood in terms of the concept of 'socialist realism', the pre-revolutionary symphonic output of the Russian Empire can be usefully approached along familiar nationalist lines, as the country strove to develop a Russian repertoire that was audibly distinct from northern European and especially German music.

The group of composers variously known as 'The Five', the 'Mighty Handful', the 'Mighty Five', and the 'New Russian School' were responsible for developing this distinctively Russian sound. They were:

◆ Mily Balakirev (1837–1910)
◆ César Cui (1835–1918)
◆ Modest Mussorgsky (1839–1881)
◆ Nicolai Rimsky-Korsakov (1844–1908)
◆ Alexander Borodin (1833–1887)

These composers strove to build on the work of the previous generation, which included **Mikhail Glinka** (1804–1857) and **Alexander Dargomyzhsky** (1813–1869). While the older generation focused on composition of Russian opera, the New Russian School put much more emphasis on instrumental music as a transcendent vehicle for Russian self-expression. For us, the crucial contributors here are Balakirev, Rimsky-Korsakov, and Borodin, but while they share a nationality and a genre, there is a large amount of diversity in their output. **Rimsky-Korsakov**, for instance, is mainly known nowadays as a programmaticist, having made regular use of folk stories and fairy tales, for example, in his symphonic suite *Scheherazade*. His three symphonies of 1861–1865, 1868 (later reclassified as a symphonic suite), and 1866–1873 are not frequently performed nowadays; however, his treatise *Основы оркестровки* (*Principles of Orchestration*) proved to be extremely influential on later generations of orchestral composers.

Balakirev's only symphony to fall within the historical limits of this book is his First Symphony in C major. The stronger emphasis on colouristic orchestration is typical of this era of Russian composition, as he uses a larger orchestra than would have been normal by Brahmsian standards, including triple woodwind, two harps, and an array of percussion instruments. Creative orchestration aside, the academic nature of the symphony that prevailed during this time is audible in the densely worked contrapuntal writing.

Perhaps the fact that **Borodin**'s musical activities were secondary to his main career as a chemist in St Petersburg meant that he felt less pressure to write in the 'academic' symphonic style. Although his first completed symphony in E♭ (the première of which was conducted by Balakirev) is much more outwardly conservative in both resource and form, his music is less reliant on thoroughgoing contrapuntal activity and harks back to the clean formal lines and transparent orchestration of the earlier part of the century. Sentential and periodic writing can regularly be found in the thematic material, giving this music a poetic quality that distinguishes it both from Brahmsian 'musical prose' and from his Russian contemporaries. His Second Symphony in B minor represents a significant progression from the earlier work, with its bold unison opening gesture and allusions to folk idioms, especially through Slavic dance rhythms in the finale, in which the notated $\frac{3}{4}$ metre is destabilised by cross-rhythms. Borodin's Third Symphony only made it to the stage of a collection of sketches, but the Russian composer **Alexander Glazunov** (1865–1936) completed and orchestrated the two-movement work, which comprises a pastoral A minor first movement and an energetic Scherzo in the unusual time signature of $\frac{5}{8}$.

Pyotr Ilyich Tchaikovsky (1840–1893) was not a member of 'The Five' but is nowadays the most well-known and undoubtedly the most frequently performed Russian composer of the nineteenth century. His symphonic output has been divided by some historians into two neat categories, with his first three numbered symphonies identified as student works and his last three as masterworks. While this is a blunt and rather old-fashioned distinction, it is nevertheless apparent that a significant change in compositional style can be heard from his Fourth Symphony onward. While Tchaikovsky, for our purposes, is probably the most important Russian symphonist, he is primarily known as a composer of ballet music. It was between his Third Symphony in D, the 'Polish', and his Fourth Symphony in F minor that he composed his first great ballet, *Swan Lake* in 1875–1876, and this clearly revolutionised his approach to instrumental composition. The frequent fugal writing in the early symphonies, especially the First and the Third, gives the impression that the hand of the conservatoire was firmly on his shoulder, resulting in an academic approach that is audible in the densely woven counterpoint that can be found throughout these works.

His later orchestral music seems to be imbued with his style of ballet composition, in which the Beethovenian technique of motivic development is often abandoned and replaced with lyrical, pictorial, or otherwise static episodes that seem to be closed off from each other, rather like the tableaux of Russian ballet. The first movement of Tchaikovsky's Sixth Symphony in B minor presents a clear example of this. The dynamic music of the primary theme and transition are reminiscent of some of the more dramatic moments in *The Sleeping Beauty* (1889), for example. Compare this music with the secondary theme, which is a sea of calm in D major beginning in bar 89. When this music returns later in the movement in bar 305 it seems to have been barely touched by the stormy entanglements of the music that preceded it. If anything, it seems to return in an even stronger state, now in B major, which prevails to the end of the movement. The lack of tonal closure here (there is no cadence in which V–I harmony supports a melodic descent to the tonic) cuts against the apparently assured secondary theme as it seems to take its time establishing itself at the end of the movement. The potential for an ironic reading should not be discounted – the idea that the music itself is presenting a critique of the formal container that it is being served in – but it is also important to consider the influence of ballet, in which ideas of tonal unity and closure of large-scale abstract structures are secondary to conveying the extra-musical story being told through dance.

Eastern Europe

Bedřich Smetana (1824–1884), like Tchaikovsky, underwent a change of style during his career. His 'Festive' Symphony was an early work that he composed in 1853, before his stylistic reorientation. After listening to Liszt's *Faust* Symphony (not really a symphony at all, but a set of three tone poems) and his tone poem *Die Ideale*, Smetana moved away from the symphony, with its

EX. 9.1 THE SWITCH BETWEEN A TWO- AND THREE-BEAT EMPHASIS IN DVOŘÁK, SYMPHONY NO. 6 IN D, OP. 60, III, BARS 1–12

academic emphasis on obligatory form and counterpoint, and began to compose in a much freer style. We now know Smetana for his overture to *The Bartered Bride* and especially for his symphonic cycle *Má Vlast* ('My Homeland'), composed in 1875, which contains the famous symphonic poem *Vltava*, named after the main river that flows through Bohemia (roughly the same territory as today's Czech Republic). The representation of national landmarks, relics, dances, and folk tunes became increasingly important as composers from countries across Europe strove to create a national style, one that was instantly recognisable and identifiable as from their homeland. *Vltava* beautifully depicts the journey of that river from source to sea, and later calls on folk tunes to illustrate typical Czech scenes including a country wedding and a dance of the water nymphs. Smetana is perhaps one of the casualties of the War of the Romantics – a composer who began in the absolute music tradition, but who was won over by the allure of the New German School and would never attempt another symphony.

Antonin Dvořák's (1841–1904) story perhaps gives a more positive impression of the symphony in the Czech lands. While his first three contributions might be considered student works, his later symphonies have proved to be enduring favourites in concert halls and on the airwaves. Like Smetana, Dvořák made use of folk tunes from his native Bohemia to bring a sense of Czech style to his symphonic output while embracing a German approach to form. Having already achieved success with his first set of *Slavonic Dances* (orchestral pieces that evoke the style of Bohemian folk music), Dvořák took a well-known folk dance, the *Furiant*, as the primary material in the third movement (a Scherzo and Trio) of his Sixth Symphony. This folk dance is characterised by regularly switching between a two-beat and three-beat emphasis. By showcasing it in his symphony Dvořák was able to symbolise national pride in what was ultimately an Austro-German form, while taking the symphony as a genre to a wider audience (**EX. 9.1**).

United States of America

Dvořák was appointed director of the National Conservatory of Music in New York in 1892 and stayed in the United States for two and a half years. He was exposed to a great deal of African American and Native American music while he was there, both from journals transcribing spirituals and from live experiences such as seeing Native American musicians performing at Buffalo Bill's 'Wild West Show'. He was called upon to combine these musical traditions with symphonic composition, developing America's own national style. On 21 May 1893, a New York Herald article quoted Dvořák's response to the music he had experienced there:

> In the Negro melodies of America, I discover all that is needed for a great and noble school of music . . . There is nothing in the whole range of composition that cannot be supplied with themes from this source. The American musician understands these tunes and they move sentiment in him.[3]

---

3   Interviewed by James Creelman, *New York Herald,* May 21, 1893.

Just a week later, an article in the same paper read 'Dr Dvořák's explicit announcement that his newly completed symphony reflects the Negro melodies, upon which . . . the coming American school must be based . . . will be a surprise to the world.'[4] This was no understatement. The influence of these spirituals can be heard clearly in the secondary theme of the first movement of 'Dr Dvořák's' Ninth Symphony, which closely resembles the famous melody of *Swing low, sweet chariot* (**EX. 9.2A** and **EX. 9.2B**).

EX. 9.2A DVOŘÁK, SYMPHONY NO. 9, I, BARS 149–152

EX. 9.2B *SWING LOW, SWEET CHARIOT*

There is no doubt that this most famous of Dvořák's later works is a clear example of his broader synthesis of irresistible melody, colouristic orchestration, and formal logic and coherence. The 'New World' Symphony, No. 9 in E minor, was hailed as 'a triumph for the sons and daughters of slavery'.[5] Some, however, saw this as a reason to be critical of Dvořák's compositional approach. **Amy Beach** (1867–1944) was sceptical about his reference to spirituals. She saw it as a form of cultural appropriation and believed composers ought to be fully immersed in a culture before daring to represent it. Beach was specifically critical of Dvořák's use of melodies originating from communities that had suffered as a result of the slave trade, writing that the Ninth Symphony depicted only 'the peaceful, sunny side of the Negro character and life. Not for a moment does it suggest their sufferings, heartbreaks, and slavery.'[6] Beach's 'Gaelic' Symphony pursued an alternative approach to Dvořák's. While Dvořák believed the concert music of America should draw on African American spirituals, Beach drew on Boston's Gaelic identity, representing a culture she was familiar with. Her symphony was premièred by the Boston Symphony Orchestra in 1896, and reimagines traditional Irish folk melodies, as well as her own folk-inspired songs. The debates and controversies surrounding the construction of an American musical style would continue into the twentieth century with the reception of music by Charles Ives (1874–1954), George Gershwin (1898–1937), and Aaron Copland (1900–1990).

4   *New York Herald*, May 28, 1893.

5   Maurice Peress, *Dvořák to Duke Ellington: a conductor explores America's music and its African American roots* (Oxford: Oxford University Press, 2004).

6   Amy Beach, 'Music reviews, vol. 2,' (October 1894), 34.

Nordic countries

Like the UK, the Nordic countries were late to catch up in terms of serious symphonic com-position, and the story here is a familiar one. While Denmark boasts an important baroque composer in **Dieterich Buxtehude** (1637–1707, who taught J. S. Bach!), a regular supply of sym-phonies was not forthcoming from the region during the eighteenth century. It was thanks to the establishment of the Leipzig Conservatoire that a means of learning the art, craft, and trade of symphonic composition became a possibility for aspiring musicians, and the 'Leipzig' style, with its emphasis on contrapuntal technique, quickly began to spread north. The Dane, **Niels Gade** (1817–1890), was an important Leipzig graduate who, along with **J.P.E. Hartmann** (1805–1900), went on to establish a conservatoire in Copenhagen. While they composed ten symphonies be-tween them (two by Hartmann and eight by Gade), the style is quite similar to Mendelssohn's.

Looking further north, the Swedish composer **Franz Berwald** (1796–1868) wrote four sym-phonies during the 1840s, after he had already established a successful orthopaedic clinic in Berlin, but before he decided to pursue a career as a glassblower in Ångermanland in northern Sweden. Between these times he visited Vienna and composed two symphonies in 1842 and another two in 1845. The most famous of these is his Third Symphony in C major, *Sinfonie Singulière*. This is a work that is well ahead of its time in many ways, not least the very romantic opening bars that fan out contrapuntally and seem to evoke something of the openness of the Swedish landscape. Berwald also deploys some formal innovations, especially by folding the slow movement and the Scherzo into one single continuous movement; the Scherzo in this case is enveloped by the slow, reflective music in the middle of this three-movement work. The symphony was not performed until long after his death in 1905.

The late-nineteenth-century flourishing of symphonic composition in the Nordic region is not, as it happens, associated with Scandinavia's most famous composer. Although the Norwegian **Edvard Grieg** (1843–1907) did compose a Symphony in C minor (1863–4), it does seem to fall into the category of a student work in which formal coherence is prized above all else, even mel-odic invention. As a Leipzig graduate, Grieg would have learned the craft in the Mendelssohnian tradition, but he went on to develop a career as a miniaturist, concentrating on songs (in Ger-man), incidental music for the theatre such as *Peer Gynt*, and short character pieces for solo piano. His Piano Concerto in A minor is his most famous work nowadays, but it is an exception.

The Nordic symphony really took off with what has come to be known as the 'Generation of 1865', named after the handful of important composers born in that year. They include the Dane, **Carl Nielsen** (1865–1931) and the Fin, **Jean Sibelius** (1865–1957). These two symphonists, both key figures in the so-called 'Nordic breakthrough', present a problem for our study. They were composing symphonies before 1900, but their careers spill into the twentieth century, with both men composing symphonic music well into the 1920s. They are also frequently paired together in recordings and concert programmes, but musically they were opposites in many respects. Nielsen was educated at Copenhagen Conservatoire and studied with Niels Gade. His musical lineage is therefore directly traceable back to the Mendelssohnian, classicis-ing approach to instrumental forms. Fugue and counterpoint more generally make a regular appearance in Nielsen's symphonies, but it is difficult to understand his music as 'romantic' in any meaningful sense. There is a classicising impulse in his approach to form, but his music, like Sibelius's, is better understood as an early contribution to twentieth-century modernism. His First Symphony was completed in 1892 and first performed in 1894. That year, the young Carl Nielsen had shown a manuscript of the work to Brahms, who he greatly admired (who wouldn't admire Brahms – the most famous living composer in Europe?!). Brahms was apparently generally approving of the younger composer's music, though the approach to tonality must have raised an eyebrow: the symphony is in G minor, but the work opens and closes in C major, putting a question to the idea of tonal unity discussed in Chapter 7.

Nielsen was reliant on folk music idioms throughout his career, and this can also be said of Sibelius. Finland was in a different political situation from Denmark. Outside of the linguistic and cultural orbit of Scandinavia, Finland was a Grand Duchy of the Russian Empire, and in the later stages of the century there was an increasing necessity for the political calls for an independent Finland to be accompanied by a genuinely Finnish expression of nationalist sentiment through music, poetry, and visual art. The Finnish national epic, the *Kalevala*, became an important text to which artists such as Akseli Gallen-Kallela and musicians like Sibelius responded. While some of Sibelius's music responds directly to this text (for instance, his *Lemminkäinen Suite*), his symphonies are sometimes thought to express something more abstract about the Finnish language, with his frequent monotone melodies ending with a downward plunge (**EX. 9.3**).

EX. 9.3 SIBELIUS, SYMPHONY NO. 2, III, BARS 146–148, MELODIC 'DOWNWARD PLUNGE'

Sibelius's compositional project seems markedly different from Nielsen's. He engaged in both tone-poem and symphonic composition. The two genres, which had been diametrically opposed during the War of the Romantics, hold equal status in his output. By the end of his career, the two modes of musical expression seemed to come together: his final one-movement Symphony in C and his last tone poem, *Tapiola*, are barely distinguishable in terms of genre.

◆　◆　◆

In this chapter we have covered a number of composers who belong to what have been called the 'European peripheries', that is, regions away from the Austro-German 'centre'. Such a description might seem slightly odd – to what extent might we consider Dvořák's 'New World' Symphony 'peripheral'? The composer we will focus on for the final chapter of this book occupies a similarly curious position. Gustav Mahler lived his life across many boundaries. His career crossed over from the nineteenth-century romantic world into twentieth-century modernism. He was born a Jew but later converted to Christianity. He lived and worked in Vienna, the centre of gravity of the Austro-German symphonic tradition, but he originally came from provincial Moravia. This makes him a fitting person with which to conclude our study, at the crossroads of symphonic composition around 1900.

10

The symphony's second age

As early as 1839 Robert Schumann was casting doubt on the future of symphonic composition, suspecting that the genre had already 'run its course'.[1] These words came from a man who had demonstrated his commitment to the classical tradition, and would go on to compose four symphonies that have all remained in the concert repertoire. Such was the downbeat mood mid-century that the predictions of the death of the genre would become a self-fulfilling prophecy. In his essay of 1851, *Opera and Drama*, Richard Wagner had, according to musicologist Carl Dahlhaus, 'pronounced the death of the symphony, viewing the post-Beethovenian efforts as a mere epilogue with nothing substantially new to say.'[2] We have seen in Chapter 9 that, while symphonies did continue to emerge during these years, many of them were student works and few composers would pursue symphonic composition in a sustained way, at least in the traditional sense. We heard how many composers, including some important nineteenth-century names such as Bizet, Smetana, Sullivan, and Grieg, would make one contribution to the genre as a student before moving on to other things. While it may have been necessary as an academic demonstration of technical ability, it would have been difficult to take such works seriously as contributions to a canon that already included large-scale works by Beethoven, Schubert, Mendelssohn, and Schumann.

Brahms had been composing during these years but had focused primarily on music at a smaller scale: piano music, chamber music, and *Lieder*. He began work on a symphony in the 1850s but its first performance would not take place until decades later. The pressure and weight of tradition by this point must have been enormous. The ambition was to compose a symphony that would be:

- substantial and serious enough to stand next to Beethoven's output
- engaging enough not to be written off as merely an academic exercise
- able to make the case in favour of the Beethovenian symphonic tradition and stand against the growing achievements of the New German School (see Chapter 8)

1876 was the year of the ideological showdown. The first complete performance of all four music dramas of Wagner's *Der Ring des Niebelungen* were given in August of that year

1   Robert Schumann, *Neue Zeitschrift für Musik*, April 20, 1839.
2   Carl Dahlhaus, *Nineteenth-Century Music* (California: University of California Press 1989), 265.

(pointedly preceded by an inaugural performance of Beethoven's Ninth Symphony at the opening of the Festspielhaus in Bayreuth). The first performances of Brahms's First Symphony were given only a few months later in November and December. According to Hepokoski, the work's 'mere appearance and obvious success served as a manifesto by example and played a prominent role in ushering in ... "the second age of the symphony".'[3]

This 'second age' was spearheaded by Brahms, but it would draw in many of the composers discussed in the previous chapter. These musicians were born around 1840 and came from diverse places across northern Europe. Along with Brahms, they included Dvořák, Bruckner, Tchaikovsky, Raff, Borodin, and others. While we sometimes think of these composers as romantics, they were in fact working after the romantic age that we would normally associate with Schubert, Mendelssohn, and Schumann in Austria and Germany, and Chopin and Berlioz in France. While these later composers wrote much of the symphonic music we would normally hear at a concert or on the radio, they occupy quite a peculiar time in music history in which this apparently dead genre was being resurrected and repurposed in concert halls around Europe. This so-called 'second age' also helped to propel the symphony into the modernist era, which was beginning to pick up pace from the late 1880s.

Gustav Mahler (1860–1911) belonged to the progressive younger generation of early-modernist composers, which also included Nielsen, Sibelius, Debussy, Strauss, Elgar, and Glazunov. This diverse group of musicians – sometimes called 'the 1865 generation' – all found themselves in a situation where they had to respond to new artistic challenges in the decades around 1900. The canon of works that would be regularly performed in concert halls across Europe had fully solidified by this time, and new compositions would need to sit next to canonical symphonies by Beethoven, Mendelssohn, Schumann, and Brahms in concert programmes. The music that the younger generation were composing was largely conceived in this context as they responded to new developments in formal construction and instrumental colour.

It was during these years that the symphony orchestra made its most significant expansion in the palette of colours available, as well as in sheer size. This is evident from simply looking at the instrumentation of some of Mahler's symphonies, which variously contain:

◆ Guitar, mandolin, cowbells (Seventh Symphony)
◆ Solo double bass (First Symphony, 'Titan', third movement)
◆ Off-stage brass (Second Symphony, finale)
◆ Large orchestra, double chorus, and six vocal soloists (Eighth Symphony)
◆ An orchestral hammer (Sixth Symphony, finale)

The percussion section also expanded significantly during this time, especially in France and Russia, and this was the era in which, about 75 years after Beethoven's Ninth Symphony, it became a much more common occurrence to find a choir and vocal soloists involved in a symphony. Four of Mahler's nine completed symphonies feature singers in one way or another, and the expansion in scale and volume tended to be concentrated in one place in particular.

---

3   Hepokoski, *A Sonata Theory Handbook*, 239.

The sense of ending

In the classical symphony, the serious music tended to be concentrated at the beginning. The first movement's sonata form would usually be the most complex structure in the work and contain the weighty ideas. These could then be departed from, or reflected on, in the slow movement before a tonal and temporal return in the Minuet. This return would then be confirmed with a finale whose materials would ordinarily be light and frothy, and couched in a form that would not be too taxing on listeners. A more straightforward sonata structure was most common, but the even simpler rondo was also a favourite. During the nineteenth century, the balance shifted decisively toward the end of the work. Opening sonata forms would frequently set a 'problem' to be solved by the remainder of the symphony. This problem often had to do with the minor mode, which the first movement had failed to escape. Beethoven's Fifth Symphony in C minor is the clearest classical example of this strategy – the heroic journey from struggle to triumph. Brahms's First Symphony presents a very interesting example in which the C minor first movement produces tonal closure in the tonic minor, but then the mood brightens in the coda to a prospective, but at this stage very speculative, C major. The finale is agonising because of continuous detours, dead ends, and insurgencies in minor keys before C major finally wins and closes the work in triumphant fashion, encapsulating the romantic idea of the hard-earned victory.

Closure really mattered to composers in the second age of the symphony. It is a simple fact that the number of cadences in large-scale compositions during this time had reduced markedly, meaning that the weight of expectation and the release of tension when a cadence does arrive is all the more satisfying. Bruckner was a master of controlling tension in his symphonies, which can last over an hour in performance. It is not uncommon to find whole movements that contain no perfect cadences at all, and his Eighth Symphony contains only one full close in the tonic, which he saves for the coda of the last movement. This shift of emphasis towards the final attainment of tonal and structural closure at the very end of a long symphonic work – sometimes called 'end-accentuation' – is a central characteristic of the late-romantic symphony, and one that Gustav Mahler took to extreme proportions in his colossal Third Symphony.

CASE STUDY: SYMPHONY NO. 3 IN D MINOR (1896) BY GUSTAV MAHLER

Mahler finished composing his Third Symphony in 1896. Individual movements would receive first performances in the following years but the first complete performance would come only in 1902 and it was later subjected to revisions by the composer. Around the time he completed the first version, Mahler claimed: 'My symphony will be something *the world has not had before!* The whole of nature finds a voice in it and reveals profound mysteries such as one might perhaps intuit in dreams!'.[4] The work is still considered the longest symphony in the regular concert repertoire and its scoring calls for one of the largest ensembles; in Mahler's output it is eclipsed only by his Eighth Symphony, nicknamed the 'Symphony of a Thousand'

---

4   Mahler in a letter to Anna von Mildenburg, July 1886. See H. Blaukopf (Ed.), *Gustav Mahler Briefe*, 165.

because of the large number of performers it requires, though Mahler never accepted that title. Mahler's Third is also set in six movements rather than the usual four. Each of these is connected through a narrative that draws on philosophical and even theological topics that convey an increasing sense of inevitability as the work progresses. There is an attempt here to combine the programmatic aspects of the story and the more abstract tonal and thematic structures with the aim of attaining both musical and narrative finality at the end.

The unity of the work hinges on a specific tonal plan that is abstract, but quite simple. The symphony as a whole charts an overarching path towards the target key of D major, which is the tonic key of the finale. While the first movement begins decisively in D minor, the main sonata form of that movement is set in F major, and it is from this embarkation point that a sequence of rising thirds unfolds, ultimately arriving back at D major in the finale where the symphony's tonal objective is finally consolidated. This abstract, tonal, upward trajectory is paired with the extra-musical ascent through the hierarchy of being, which takes us on a journey somewhat resembling the Christian creation story.

TABLE 10.1 OVERARCHING PLAN OF MAHLER'S SYMPHONY NO. 3

No. 1	No. 2	No. 3	No. 4	No. 5	No. 6
Introduction – 'Pan Awakens' – 'Summer Marches In'	'What the Flowers of the Field Tell Me'	'What the Beasts of the Woods Tell Me'	'What Man Tells Me'	'What the Angels Tell Me'	'What Love Tells Me'
Large sonata form	Minuet	Scherzando	Slow, misterioso with alto solo	Upbeat choral movement	Adagio
D minor – F major	A major	C minor	D major	F major	D major

Similar to his First and Second Symphonies, Mahler drew on his own previous output for the Third. His set of songs, *Des Knaben Wunderhorn*, forms a backdrop to these early symphonies. Direct quotations from this set of songs are readily apparent in these works. The ethos of song as a guiding principle is notable in Mahler's Third, especially in the later stages of the work; this period of Mahler's creative activity has been characterised as 'symphonic song' similar to the way that Wagner's music dramas can be understood as 'symphonic opera'.[5]

The programmatic idea behind the work hinges on the progress through ever higher states of being. Mahler invites us to hear the symphony this way by assigning titles to each of the movements in a similar way to Beethoven in his 'Pastoral' Symphony. The six movements of the symphony are organised into two parts, with Part 1 consisting only of the gigantic first movement and Part 2 comprising the remaining five movements. The journey from abstraction, through plant and animal life and then to mankind and beyond, is clear from this plan, but it is made even clearer when we consider that in an earlier version the first movement had been

5   Friedrich Saathen, Preface to *Mahler, Symphony III*, (London: Universal Edition, 1974), v–viii.

called 'What the Mountainside Tells Me', suggesting the image of the rocks and stones of the mountains as yet a lower state of being than the flowers in the field.

The symphony is also notable for its diversity of content. Mahler claimed in 1907 (in a conversation with Sibelius no less!) that '[t]he symphony must be like the world. It must embrace everything.'[6] Even by this visionary standard the Third Symphony seems to exceed expectations. Each of the six movements seems to draw on different materials, and even different musical traditions and practices. The first movement – which takes longer than half an hour to play – draws initially on funeral music and then, increasingly, on military styles, all of which point towards the march topic (see Chapter 2), now reimagined in the 1890s. The essence of the march is unchanged after a hundred years, and bears comparison with Haydn's 'Military' Symphony, No. 100 in G major. Duple metre, a quick tempo, and use of the recognised 'military' instruments (flute, trumpet, drums) all remain in place. As you can see from the musical examples, though, the execution had changed drastically (**EX. 10.1** and **EX. 10.2**).

The second movement draws most obviously on the Minuet tradition of the classical symphony, contrasting with the folk-influenced third movement (drawing on the *Wunderhorn* song 'Ablösung im Sommer'), the calm religiosity of the fourth, and the appeal to children's music and nursery rhymes in the fifth, which also takes its text and much of the musical material from the *Wunderhorn* songs 'Das himmlische Leben' and 'Es Sungen Drei Engel' (**EX. 10.3** and **EX. 10.4**).[7]

The ascent through the hierarchy of being is supported by the inclusion of vocalists in movements four and five. The alto soloist in the fourth movement sings the 'Midnight' song from Friedrich Nietzsche's philosophical novel *Also Sprach Zarathustra*:

Original Text	English Translation
O Mensch! Gib Acht!	O Man! Take heed!
Was spricht die tiefe Mitternacht?	What does the deep midnight say?
'Ich schlief, ich schlief –	I slept! I slept,
Aus tiefem Traum bin ich erwacht: –	I have awoken from deep dreaming
Die Welt ist tief,	The world is deep!
Und tiefer als der Tag gedacht.	And deeper than the day conceives!
[O Mensch! O Mensch!]	O man! O man!
Tief ist ihr Weh –	Deep! Deep is its woe!
Lust — tiefer noch als Herzeleid;	Joy, joy deeper still than heart-ache!
Weh spricht; Vergeh!	Woe says: be lost!
Doch alle Lust will Ewigkeit –	But all joy wills eternity! –
– will tiefe, tiefe Ewigkeit!'	Wills deep, deep eternity![8]

6   Cited in Norman Lebrecht, *Mahler Remembered* (London: Faber & Faber, 1987), 218.

7   Constantin Floros, *Gustav Mahler III: Die Symphonien* (Wiesbaden: Breitkopf & Härtel, 1985); tr. Vernon and Jutta Wicker as *Gustav Mahler: The Symphonies* (Pompton Pains and Cambridge: Amadeus Press, 1993), 92.

8   Translation reproduced from Peter Franklin, *Mahler: Symphony No. 3* (Cambridge: Cambridge University Press, 1991), 67.

EX. 10.1 HAYDN, SYMPHONY NO. 100 IN G, 'MILITARY', II, BARS 152–164

EX. 10.2 MAHLER, SYMPHONY NO. 3, I, BARS 315–319, 'IMMER DASSELBE TEMPO'

Here, the jump from purely instrumental music to vocal music and, crucially, language expresses the progression from flowers and beasts (the lower levels of the hierarchy) to humans. The motion from the deep philosophising of humanity in the fourth movement to the nonsensical 'Bimm, bamm, bimm, bamm' of the children's choir imitating bell sounds in the fifth movement (**EX. 10.3**), announcing the arrival of the angels, initiates the next part of the ascent through the hierarchy of being. The text and music – another song from *Des Knaben Wunderhorn* (**EX. 10.4**) – is not concerned with the entanglements of 'joy' and 'woe' that the alto had been concerned with in the fourth movement, nor is it couched in Nietzsche's atheist worldview. It is an overtly Christian text with the message that salvation is assured through God's love. This short choral movement sets up the final motion through the hierarchy in which text and language are no longer sufficient as a means of expression. The all-important finale combines low and high styles with a choral-style theme (though it only uses instruments, in similar fashion to Brahms' First Symphony or Saint-Saëns' Third). This is a critical moment in the symphony, which sets it apart from other choral–symphonic works.

From the time of Beethoven's Ninth Symphony, the idea of the choral finale was key because it presented the message that you can only go so far with instruments alone and that at a certain critical moment it is necessary to burst into song, first pronounced when the baritone soloist in the finale sings, 'Oh friends, not these sounds!' (*O Freunde, nicht diese töne!*). Even in apparently purely abstract symphonies like Brahms's First, the finale's primary theme resembles choral music, and brings with it an important political message of unity. In Mahler's Third, however, the message is much more radical: the hierarchy of being as the composer conceived it began with instrumental expression, progressed upward to language at the human and superhuman levels, and then finally through language altogether – as if to go *out the other side of it* – to a yet higher form of purely instrumental expression that has the ability to incorporate all that had gone before it, reconciling the challenges and anomalies, and marshalling all those forces to come to a more profound finality.

This finality is expressed in a highly unusual way. The symphony's final movement is not the fast-paced sonata structure that was the normal choice for late-nineteenth-century works, but rather an Adagio. It was therefore one of the first slow finales in the repertoire. It is relatively straightforward in its overarching formal plan, a set of episodic variations in ABABA form. The goal of the movement's tonal trajectory, D major, is proposed by the theme at the start of the movement, but it is repeatedly displaced by an antagonistic C♯ minor. The question that this movement asks, in purely musical terms, is whether it is possible to achieve a D major cadence that will not be undermined, and which can be sustained until the end. The answer, in this case, is an emphatic yes. After three progressively intense moments of crisis and collapse (bars 71–91, 182–197, and 220–244), the increasingly confident and richly orchestrated D major theme picks itself up (originally written for strings but in bar 252 rescored for trumpets with string support), and slowly but surely builds towards the climactic moment of tonal closure that the movement – and the whole symphony – has been moving towards: the D major perfect cadence at bar 400. This cadence, unlike previous attempts in the movement, is underlined by the cymbals and bass drum, giving the moment of punctuation an extra element of sonic sturdiness. Unlike the theme's previous attempts to secure D major, this one prevails to the end of the work, which closes with a massively expanded plagal (IV–I) motion which also underscores the quasi-religious subject of the work.

EX. 10.4 MAHLER, *ES SUNGEN DREI ENGEL* FROM *DES KNABEN WUNDERHORN*, BARS 1–13

◆　◆　◆

The transformation that the symphony underwent from its origins in the opera house and the theatre to the colossal works of the 1890s is difficult to overstate. The formal design, tonal space, and performing forces had all undergone revolutionary growth over the years, but the factors that shaped the genre – the institutions, political ideas, systems of patronage, national styles, aesthetic debates and controversies, and the voices of individual composers – meant that the development during this 150-year period, from the sinfonia a 8 to the modernist symphony orchestra, was far from smooth. It is tempting to talk of 'the standard symphony orchestra', though such a thing really does not exist. There were conventions (two clarinets, three trombones, and so on), but it is quite difficult to point even to a single decade in which the make-up of the orchestra was constant or standardised. What can be said of the instrumentation of these works can also be said about their scope, scale, and meaning. In many respects, the symphony remains difficult to define in anything but the loosest terms. 'The coming together of all the resources of music' might be one attempt, drawing on the etymology of the word: 'sym' meaning 'together' and 'phony' meaning 'sound', but this seems to miss much of what the symphonic tradition is about. This definition also collapses the various debates, controversies, ruptures, discontinuities, and contradictions that are evident from music history and which can be *heard* in the repertoire.

The heights reached by Mahler in the 1890s and 1900s are regularly read in popular commentaries as the end of a tradition, as if Mahler was the last romantic symphonist, and that the Beethovenian tradition he represented would soon be overtaken by a number of '-isms' – modernism, neo-classicism, expressionism, symbolism – that had been gathering momentum. It is true to say that Mahler's symphonies are the longest and largest in the regular concert repertoire, but this is not evidence that the symphonic tradition was abandoned after his death in 1911. Mahler's legacy was felt strongly in subsequent decades. Within Austria and Germany his expansion of the tonal palette was influential for the new generation of modernists, who included Schoenberg, Webern, and Berg. Though it is difficult to see any similarity between Mahler's output and Webern's tiny Symphony, Op. 21, which takes only 10 minutes to play, it is difficult to imagine Webern creating that work without the long tradition that had been built up, the expanded tonal palette that Mahler had been cultivating, and the rebellion against the symphonic inheritance that Webern was expressing. Likewise, it would be difficult to imagine the continuation of the symphonic tradition outside of Austria and Germany without Mahler's influence. The blend of romanticism with ideas drawn from modernism and national styles was absolutely essential in the UK (Elgar, Vaughan Williams, Walton), the Nordic region (Sibelius, Nielsen), and Russia (Shostakovich, Prokofiev) in the first half of the twentieth century.

Ultimately, the symphony remains difficult to distil into a neat definition, and the repertoire is characterised more by its diversity than by its uniformity. It can be helpful – even necessary, sometimes – to bring our own expectations to the listening experience. Without the expectation of a four-movement work with a fast finale, for example, how could we register the slow finish to Mahler's Third Symphony as something unusual? Without the knowledge of the programme of *Harold en Italie*, is it possible to have a full and complete listening experience? Without an understanding of galant style, is it possible to fully appreciate Mozart's 'Jupiter'

Symphony? In other words, this is a repertoire that repays study and asks for an investment from us as listeners and performers. Against the odds, though, and through all the ruptures and upheavals of the nineteenth century, the symphony has survived, and it remains one of the central repertoires in concert halls today.

POINTS FOR FURTHER DISCUSSSION

- Discuss Berlioz's use of programmatic writing in his *Symphonie Fantastique*.
- What were the challenges facing symphonic composers in the nineteenth century?
- Why is the programme/absolute music debate important when discussing the development of the symphony?
- To what extent is the symphony an Austro-German genre?
- Is it accurate to describe Dvorak's Ninth Symphony as a European symphony?
- To what extent is the symphony an eighteenth-century genre?
- How did Beethoven cast a shadow over symphonic composers in the nineteenth century?
- How useful are terms such as 'classical' and 'romantic' when discussing the symphony from 1750-1900?

Glossary

Absolute music	Music that does not express non-musical ideas.
Antecedent	The first part of a musical period. A basic idea is continued towards an imperfect cadence.
Biedermeier Vienna	The predominantly middle-class culture that was dominant in Vienna from the end of the Napoleonic Wars until the 1848 Revolutions.
Binary form	A movement organised into two sections, usually separated by a double bar, in which the first moves away from the tonic to establish a new key and the second returns to and confirms the initial tonic. Both sections are usually repeated.
Cadential deferral	The process by which tonal closure is postponed to a later stage in a piece of music.
Canon	A small body of repertoire that has become dominant over time. Sometimes these works are characterised as 'masterpieces' and are regarded as timeless.
Central action	The middle part of the development section of a sonata form, usually involving a climax.
Circle of fifths	Harmonic motion by successive intervals of a fifth in the bass voice.
Closing zone	The final stage of a sonata exposition or recapitulation in which the key of the secondary theme (and its associated perfect cadence) is confirmed and reinforced.
Coda	A passage of music that occurs after the end of a musical form (such as a rondo or a sonata form). Its function is to frame or to round off an already completed musical form.
Col legno	'With the wood' – an instruction for string players to use the wood of the bow instead of the hair.
Concertino	A small group of soloists within a larger ensemble.
Concerto	An extensive work for a solo instrument or group of soloists that contrast with an orchestra.
Concerto grosso	An orchestral work written for a small group of soloists (concertino) against a full orchestra (ripieno).
Consequent	The second part of a musical period. The basic idea is continued towards a perfect cadence.

Counterpoint	A texture in which two or more melodies play against each other.
Cycle	The organisation of the movements of a large-scale work such as a symphony.
Cyclical form	The structure of a multi-movement work such as a symphony in which material first heard at the beginning returns in later movements, especially in the finale.
Developing variation	A technique associated with the music of Brahms in which small motivic units are subtly and continuously varied in order to produce the effect of thematic transformation.
Development	The middle section of a sonata form in which the return of the primary theme and the tonic key is delayed and in which the thematic material is developed and reorganised.
End-accentuation	The musical, structural or rhetorical emphasis is found at the end of the piece or section rather than the opening.
Enharmonic seam	In tonal music the invisible borderline between the sharp keys and the flat keys. If a composer is writing in F♯ and then begins to renotate the same pitches in G♭ then the music has 'crossed the enharmonic seam'.
Exposition	The first section of a sonata form in which the themes chart a path from tonic to dominant (or another related key).
Expressionism	A short-lived style of modernism found in music and especially visual art in the years before the First World War in which explosive emotions seem to warp or distort conventional imagery or musical structures.
Form	The internal organisation of individual movements.
Formenlehre	The 'teaching of musical form'. A branch of music theory in the nineteenth century concerned with the study of musical form.
Fortspinnung	Literally the 'spinning forth' of musical ideas. A common eighteenth-century compositional technique in which perpetual motion and sequences are used to propel the music towards a cadence.
Fragmentation	A characteristic of musical syntax (usually found in the continuation phase of a musical sentence) in which the basic idea is broken down into its constituent motivic units.
Fugue	An imitative contrapuntal texture in which successive voices enter with a statement of the basic idea alternately on I and V.
Galant style	An elegant, urbane, courtly musical style in the mid-eighteenth century that relied on a collection of recognised patterns known as 'schemata'.
Gesamtkunstwerk	'Total work of art' combining many different art forms (e.g. drama, poetry, music, costume, scenery).

Heroic tradition	The tradition of symphonic composition in the nineteenth century that drew influence from Beethoven's middle-period works, especially the Third and Fifth Symphonies.
Idée fixe	Associated with Berlioz, a theme which represents the main character or mood of a composition and which returns throughout, usually in a modified form.
Imitation	One voice in a polyphonic texture repeating material previously heard in another voice. The repetition can be at pitch or in transposition.
Imperfect cadence	An arrival on a root-position V chord that produces a limited sense of finality.
Kapellmeister	A prominent role in courts across Europe that could include directing ensembles, composing music, and teaching members of the household.
Key	A hierarchical arrangement of tones and chords that relate to a governing tonic.
Klang	A compound sound consisting of pitches within a chord combined with a particular timbre.
Mannheim *crescendo*	A *crescendo* played by the full orchestra, often with instruments added to the texture to help achieve the gradual increase in volume.
Mannheim hammer strokes	Chords played in rhythmic unison, often heard before the thematic material begins.
Mannheim rocket	An ascending, accelerating scale
Mannheim *Walze*/ roller	A musical effect used by the Mannheim school in the eighteenth century and later assimilated into orchestral works across Europe: a rising melody heard over a tonic pedal to build tension.
Minuet and trio	An eighteenth-century dance in triple metre. It is frequently used as the third movement of a symphony, and sometimes as the second movement (in which case the slow movement would be in third place).
Modernism	A group of progressive artistic movements in the late nineteenth and early twentieth centuries that sought to reorganise artistic materials in new and revolutionary ways.
Modulation	See 'tonicisation'
Monothematic	A technique used by Haydn in which the primary theme returns in the dominant key during a sonata exposition instead of a new secondary theme.
Neapolitan	The flattened supertonic (flattened second degree of the scale). This can be expressed as a triad (in the key of C, this would be a chord of D♭ major); this is always a major triad and is characteristically presented in first inversion.

Neoclassicism	A movement in the twentieth century in which classical and baroque structures and characteristics were incorporated into modernist music
New German School	The group of progressive mid-nineteenth-century composers associated with Weimar. The most important figures in this movement were Liszt and Wagner.
Obbligato	An essential instrumental part which plays counterpoint against the ensemble or another soloist.
Opera	A dramatic work set to music, largely comprising vocal and choral pieces accompanied by an orchestra.
Patronage	Support offered by wealthy individuals or institutions to musicians by means of money and/or access to resources.
Perfect cadence	A closing gesture in which a root-position V harmony moves to root-position I. The greatest degree of finality is produced when the melody approaches the tonic by step (either via the supertonic or the leading note).
Period	A unit of musical syntax consisting of two components, an antecedent and a consequent.
Portamento	A smooth slide from one note to another.
Preparation zone	An early stage in the development section of a sonata form. Usually the primary theme is heard here away from the tonic.
Primary theme	The opening theme of a sonata form which is first heard in the tonic key.
Programme music	Music that involves allusions or specific references to extra-musical ideas. These are often drawn from literary sources.
Recapitulation	The final part of a sonata form in which the themes are presented in the tonic key.
Retransition	The motion towards the tonic after time spent away from that key.
Ripieno	Full orchestra (usually string orchestra with continuo but sometimes including woodwind and brass).
Ripieno concerto	A work written for ripieno orchestra with no clear solo passages.
Romanticism	Term used to describe art music written in the period c. 1830–1900 that prioritised emotional expression.
Rondo form	A type of movement usually used for the finale of a symphony, characterised by the frequent repetition of its main theme.
Rounded binary form	A combination of binary and ternary principles which is used as a building block for larger structures such as rondos or minuets. Like binary form, it is structured in two parts, but the opening idea returns at the end.
Scherzo	A fast dance usually in compound duple or compound triple metre. The Scherzo largely replaced the Minuet in the nineteenth-century symphony.

Secondary theme	The theme heard later in the exposition of a sonata form which is presented in the dominant (or other related) key, usually producing a perfect cadence in that key. The secondary theme is played in the tonic in the recapitulation.
Sentence	A unit of musical syntax consisting of the presentation of a basic idea, its continuation, and a cadence.
Sequential motion	Repetition of a musical idea either a step higher or lower. Performing this operation more than once produces a chain of sequences.
Sinfonia	An instrumental piece used as an introduction or interlude in operas and other large-scale theatrical or sacred works.
Sinfonia a 8	A common configuration of the early symphony consisting of eight parts – 1st violins, 2nd violins, violas, cellos/basses, two oboes, and two horns.
Sonata da camera	Literally 'chamber sonata', a series of dances written for a secular setting.
Sonata di chiesa	Literally 'church sonata', a series of abstract movements written to suit the religious setting.
Sonata form	Broadly speaking, a form in which a movement is divided into (usually) three sections: exposition, development, and recapitulation. Most commonly found in first movements of symphonies and sonatas in the eighteenth and nineteenth centuries.
Symbolism	A style of musical modernism in which the functional interaction of tones, chords, and keys is replaced by fixed musical symbols.
Ternary form	A movement organised into three sections. The first section (A) is usually closed in the tonic key. This is contrasted with a central (B) section, often open-ended, before a return to (A), sometimes in a modified, varied, or otherwise developed form.
Tonal antagonism	The tension caused by disruptive pitch content within thematic material and the working-out of such tension.
Tonal escapism	The presentation of positive, lyrical, dreamy or relaxed emotional states in a key away from the tonic. $\flat$VI was a favourite choice of Schubert's.
Tonality	A system of pitch organisation in which each of the 12 chromatic tones are organised into a hierarchy of major and minor scales and keys.
Tone poem/ symphonic poem (*Tondichtung*)	A large-scale work for orchestra in one movement (or sometimes more than one movement) based on an extra-musical idea.
Tonic	The first degree of the key (or the triad built on that note), providing the harmonic point of reference in a piece of tonal music.

Tonicisation	The use of accidentals to give the impression that a particular tone is operating temporarily as a new tonic.
Transition	The part of a sonata exposition or recapitulation that connects the primary theme and the secondary theme. The transition usually modulates from tonic to dominant in sonata expositions, and usually remains in the tonic in recapitulations.
Trio sonata	A multi-movement instrumental work written for two treble instruments (usually two violins) and basso continuo.
Unending melody	A style of melodic writing regularly found in Wagner's music dramas characterised by a lack of cadential closure.
Variation form	A movement in which an initial theme is subjected to a series of increasingly varied repetitions.

Bibliography

Adorno, T. W., *Mahler: A Musical Physiognomy*, tr. E. Jophcott (Chicago: University of Chicago Press, 1996).

Agawu, V. K., *Playing with Signs: A Semiotic Interpretation of Classic Music* (Princeton: Princeton University Press, 1991).

Anderson, E., *The Letters of Mozart and His Family*, 2nd Ed. Vol. 2. (New York: St. Martin's Press, 1966).

Bauman, T., 'Mahler in a New Key: Genre and the Resurrection Finale', *The Journal of Musicology* 23/3 (2006), 468–85.

Bonds, M. E., 'Sinfonia anti-eroica: Berlioz's *Harold en Italie* and the Anxiety of Beethoven's Influence', *The Journal of Musicology* 10/4 (1992), 417–63.

Burnham, S., *Beethoven Hero* (Princeton: Princeton University Press, 1995).

Caplin, W. E., *Classical Form* (Oxford: Oxford University Press, 1998).

Caplin, W. E., J. Hepokoski, and J. Webster, *Musical Form, Forms and Formenlehre*, ed. Pieter Bergé (Leuven: Leuven University Press, 2009).

Clark, S., *Analyzing Schubert* (Cambridge: Cambridge University Press, 2011).

Dahlhaus, C., *Foundations of Music History* (Cambridge: Cambridge University Press, 1983).

——, *Nineteenth-Century Music* (California: University of California Press, 1989).

——, *The Idea of Absolute Music*, tr. R. Lustig (Chicago: University of Chicago Press, 1991).

Downes, S., *The Muse as Eros* (Aldershot: Ashgate, 2006).

Downes, S. (Ed.), *Aesthetics of Music: Musicological Perspectives* (London: Routledge, 2014).

Floros, C., *Gustav Mahler III: Die Symphonien* (Wiesbaden: Breitkopf & Härtel, 1985); tr. Vernon and Jutta Wicker as *Gustav Mahler: The Symphonies* (Pompton Pains and Cambridge: Amadeus Press, 1993).

Franklin, P., *Mahler: Symphony No. 3* (Cambridge: Cambridge University Press, 1991).

Frisch, W., *Brahms and the Principle of Developing Variation* (Berkeley: University of California Press, 1992).

Frisch, W., *Brahms: The Four Symphonies* (New York: Schirmer, 1996).

Gjerdingen, R. O., *Music in the Galant Style* (New York: Oxford University Press USA, 2007).

Goehr, L., *The Imaginary Museum of Musical Works*, revised edition (Oxford: Oxford University Press, 2001).

Grimes, N., and A. R. Mace, *Mendelssohn Perspectives* (Abingdon: Routledge, 2012).

Hanslick, E., *On The Musically Beautiful*, tr. Geoffrey Payzant (Indianapolis: Hackett, 1986).

Hepokoski, J., 'Beethoven reception: the symphonic tradition' in *The Cambridge History of Nineteenth-Century Music*, Ed. Jim Samson (Cambridge: Cambridge University Press, 2001), 424–459.

—, *A Sonata Theory Handbook* (Oxford: Oxford University Press USA, 2021).

Hepokoski J., and Darcy, W., *Elements of Sonata Theory* (Oxford: Oxford University Press, 2006).

Holoman, D. K. (Ed.), *The Nineteenth-Century Symphony* (Belmont: Wadsworth, 1996).

Horton, J, 'Bruckner's Symphonies and Sonata Deformation Theory', *Journal for the Society of Musicology in Ireland* 1 (2005), 5–17.

Horton, J. (Ed.), *The Cambridge Companion to The Symphony* (Cambridge: Cambridge University Press, 2013).

Jackson, T. L. and P. Hawkshaw (Eds), *Bruckner Studies* (Cambridge: Cambridge University Press, 1997).

Kinderman, W. and H. Krebs (Eds), *The Second Practice of Nineteenth-Century Tonality* (University of Nebraska Press, 1996).

Kramer, L., *Music as Cultural Practice, 1800–1900* (Berkeley: University of California Press, 1990).

Lawson, C., *Mozart Clarinet Concerto* (Cambridge: Cambridge University Press, 1996).

Lebrecht, N., *Mahler Remembered* (London: Faber & Faber, 1987).

McClary, S., 'Constructions of Subjectivity in Schubert's Music' in *Queering the Pitch*, ed. P. Brett, E. Wood and G. C. Thomas (Routledge, 1994), 205–234.

Mahler, G., *Zweite Symphonie* (Leipzig: Universal, 1897).

Micznik, V., 'The Absolute Limitations of Programme Music: The case of Liszt's "Die Ideale"', *Music & Letters* 80 (1999), 207–40.

Monahan, S., 'Success and Failure in Mahler's Sonata Recapitulations', *Music Theory Spectrum* 33/1 (2011).

Monahan, S., *Mahler's Symphonic Sonatas* (New York: Oxford University Press, 2015).

Newcomb, A., 'Once more "Between Absolute and Programme Music": Schumann's Second Symphony', *19th-Century Music* 7 (1983–4), 233–50.

Notley, M., '"Volksconcerte" in Vienna and Late Nineteenth-Century Ideology of the Symphony', *Journal of the American Musicological Society* 50/2, 3 (1997).

Pereira, A., *Beethoven's Dedications* (Abingdon and New York: Taylor & Francis, 2020)

Peress, M., *Dvořák to Duke Ellington: a conductor explores America's music and its African American roots* (Oxford: Oxford University Press, 2004).

Ratner, L. G., *Classic Music: Expression, Form, and Style* (London: Collier and Macmillan, 1980).

Riley, M., 'Sonata Principles', *Music & Letters* 89/4 (2008), 590–598.

—, *The Viennese Minor-Key Symphony in the Age of Haydn and Mozart* (Oxford: Oxford University Press, 2014).

Rosen, C., *The Classical Style* (London/New York: W. W. Norton & Company, 1971, repr. 1998).

Saathen, F., *Preface to Mahler, Symphony III* (London: Universal Edition, 1974).

Schmalfeldt, J., *In the Process Of Becoming* (New York: Oxford University Press USA, 2011).

Schubart, C.F.D., *Ideen zu einer Äesthetik der Tonkunst*, ed. L. Schubart (Vienna: J. V. Degen, 1806, repr. Leipzig: Reclam, 1977).

Schumann, R., *Neue Zeitschrift für Musik*, 20 April 1839.

Schumann, R., 'A Symphony by Berlioz', in *Berlioz: Fantastic Symphony*, ed. E. T. Cone (New York: W. W. Norton & Company, 1971), 220–48.

Sly, G., 'Schubert's Innovations in Sonata Form: Compositional Logic and Structural Interpretation', *Journal of Music Theory* 45/i, 119–50.

Tarrant, C., 'Structural Acceleration in Nielsen's *Sinfonia Espansiva*' in *Music Analysis* 38/iii (2019), 358–86.

Taruskin, R., *Defining Russia Musically* (Princeton: Princeton University Press, 1997).

——, *Music in the Seventeenth and Eighteenth Centuries* (Oxford: Oxford Univeristy Press, 2009).

——, *Music in the Nineteenth Century* (Oxford: Oxford University Press, 2009).

Webster, J., 'Haydn's Aesthetics' in Caryl Clark, ed., *The Cambridge Companion to Haydn* (Cambridge: Cambridge University Press, 2005).

Wingfield, P., 2008: 'Beyond "Norms and Deformations": Towards a Theory of Sonata Form as Reception History', *Music Analysis* 27/i, 137–77.

Zaslaw, N. 'Mozart's Paris Symphonies', *The Musical Times* 119/1627 (1978), 753–7.

Zaslaw, N., *Mozart's Symphonies: Context, Performance Practice, Reception* (Oxford: Oxford University Press, 1989).